CIVIL WAR RECIPES

CIVIL WAR

RECIPES

*Receipts from
the Pages of
Godey's Lady's Book*

COMPILED AND EDITED BY

LILY MAY SPAULDING AND
JOHN SPAULDING

THE UNIVERSITY PRESS OF KENTUCKY

Publication of this volume was made possible in part
by a grant from the National Endowment for the Humanities.

Copyright © 1999 by
The University Press of Kentucky
Scholarly publisher for the Commonwealth,
serving Bellarmine College, Berea College,
Centre College of Kentucky, Eastern Kentucky University,
The Filson Club Historical Society, Georgetown College,
Kentucky Historical Society, Kentucky State University,
Morehead State University, Murray State University,
Northern Kentucky University, Transylvania University,
University of Kentucky, University of Louisville,
and Western Kentucky University.

EDITORIAL AND SALES OFFICES
The University Press of Kentucky
663 South Limestone Street
Lexington, Kentucky 40508-4008

03 02   5 4 3

Civil War recipes : receipts from the pages of Godey's lady's book / compiled and
    edited by Lily May Spaulding and John Spaulding.
        p.   cm.
    Includes bibliographical references and index.
    ISBN 0-8131-2082-9 (hardcover : alk. paper)
    1. Cookery, American.   2. United States—History.—Civil War, 1861-1865.
I. Spaulding, Lily May, 1920- .   II.   Spaulding, John, 1944- .   III. Godey's
magazine.
TX715.C57427   1998
641.5973'09034—dc21   98-34445

This book is printed on acid-free recycled paper
meeting the requirements of the American National Standard
for Permanence of Paper for Printed Library Materials.

Manufactured in the United States of America

DEDICATED TO THE MEMORY OF

SARAH MAYO MOXLEY

(1880-1969)

‍CONTENTS ‍

PREFACE

LILY MAY SPAULDING

My interest in the culinary arts stems from my childhood in the 1920s. When I was nine I made my first pie (Vermont currant), which ultimately slid through a pie holder bottom side up on the kitchen floor. My mother was my baking teacher, and she in turn was taught by a pastry chef at the Woodstock Inn in Woodstock, Vermont. But her expertise extended beyond baking. In the early 1920s she made her own packaged potato chips (Green Mountain Potato Chips) and wild strawberry preserves which she sold to the Farm and Garden Shop in Boston. So, much of my interest in cooking came from her. I have always treasured her old recipes and continue to use many of them: mincemeat, mustard pickle, graham yeast bread, and boiled cider pie, to name a few.

Over the years I have been looking for an old English plum pudding recipe like the one my grandmother used to make and send to us each Christmas. It was, of course, an English pudding, as her original home was in Coventry, England, and her family did not emigrate until 1887. My son John acquired an 1863 *Godey's Lady's Book* and began searching through it. This led to our quest for other issues of *Godey's* from the Civil War period. We then realized how much it would mean to others with similar interests to preserve some of these fascinating recipes and the methods of cooking associated with this period in history. And so this book was born.

Sarah Josepha Hale

INTRODUCTION

JOHN SPAULDING

The recipes included here were selected from *Godey's Lady's Book* in the period of the Civil War, the 1860s, when the magazine was at its zenith. *Godey's Lady's Book,* perhaps the most popular magazine for women in the nineteenth century, existed in various forms for sixty-eight years, from 1830 to 1898. Unlike most American periodicals of the time, *Godey's* had a national rather than regional readership and reached its highest circulation of some 150,000 copies during the 1860s. Now famous for its hand-colored fashion plates, *Godey's* also included sections on domestic architecture, sewing patterns, fiction, science, editorials, poetry, and activities for youth, in addition to a "Receipts" column. The magazine was founded by Louis Godey, and it achieved its widest readership during the tenure of Sarah Josepha Hale, who served as editor from 1837 to 1877.

Hale began a career as an editor when she was in her forties. A remarkable woman, she was responsible for initiating the campaign to establish Thanksgiving as a national holiday and was an ardent supporter of the rights of women. She was among the first to advocate women as teachers in American public schools, and she started the first day nursery in the United States, championed the fight for retention of property rights by married women, advocated medical education for women, founded a society for increasing women's wages, and coined the term "domestic science" as part of her fight to elevate housekeeping to a profession. She established many departments in *Godey's*, including the recipe section, which appears to have been the first such section in an American women's magazine. Among her many publications are at least two books of recipes and other aspects of domestic science.

The magazine targeted women in the expanding middle class of the mid-nineteenth century. These were the wives not only of doctors, lawyers, ministers, bankers, newspaper editors, teachers, merchants, prosperous farmers, and storekeepers but also of master craftsmen such as carpenters, blacksmiths, and ironmongers, middle managers in factories and large stores, and even skilled craftsmen such as journeyman machinists and patternmakers. The middle class included up to 40 percent of the population and owned perhaps half the wealth. The average middle-class family might own their own house and have one servant (Rorabaugh, 1987).

The American middle class was in transition between the self-sufficiency of the family in the first half of the nineteenth century and the changes wrought by the economic expansion and industrialization of the second half of the century, which allowed women more leisure time. Middle-class women had been taught as young girls to draw, play the piano, crochet, and design "female elegancies" that could be displayed around the house (*Godey's* published many patterns for the latter). In the first half of the century, many women had, of course, woven cloth and sewn clothes for their families (Clark, 1987). They were now just beginning to aspire to more "cultivated" pursuits, to pay more attention to fashion, etiquette, home decoration, and cuisine—pursuits that would come to fruition in what we now think of as the style and the excesses of the Victorian age.

Meats and baked goods predominated in the average American diet of the mid-century. Although meat was scarce in the South during the war, beef and pork were heavily favored, as is reflected in the number of beef and pork recipes here. (The largest number of meat recipes found in the magazine during this decade are for beef, followed by pork, then veal, wildfowl, chicken and turkey, lamb, and wild game.) In rural areas people grew their own vegetables—potatoes, cabbages, onions, turnips, and others. Fresh vegetables were not usually available in the winter (vegetables were dried or kept in root cellars), and the diet typically included little fruit except apples. Although the North had dairies, milk consumption nationally was less than half a pint a day (McIntosh, 1995). The alcoholic beverage favored by Americans in mid-century was beer, followed by whiskey and wine (Rorabaugh, 1987).

As the following quotation from the magazine makes clear, the recipes of *Godey's* were intended for the family meals of middle-class households, not for banquets or exhibitions of *haute cuisine:* "Our *Lady's Book* receipts deal less with grand dishes for high-company occasions, and more with the common dishes of every day. . . . The dinner may be of scraps, but those scraps must be savory; and certainly the receipts and directions for turning stale crusts into delicate puddings, morsels of cold, dry meat into delicate entrees, leave cooks and wives without excuses for 'banyan days' or hungry dinners. No one can read the *Lady's Book* receipts without being struck by the good sense that pervades them as a general rule" (January 1863: 88).

Many of the recipes appearing in the magazine were contributed by its readers; others were probably contributed by Hale. Possibly because they were readers' favorites, many were repeated over the years. Because *Godey's* was a national publication, there is every reason to believe that the contributed recipes came from every region of the country; however, since the magazine was published in Philadelphia, it is unlikely that during most of the 1860s there were many contributors from the South. Nonetheless, there are certainly southern recipes here, and, taken as a whole, the recipes reflect the varying tastes and differences characteristic of the nation in mid-nineteenth century before the "melting pot" and improved communication and transportation homogenized our regional differences. The German or French potato soup had not yet become the American vichyssoise, English puddings retained their local differences, and a "Bengal recipe" for watermelon sherbet was still an exotic wonder.

The flavor of the immigrant nature of our country in the 1860s is present in the names of the recipes themselves; the following countries are specifically mentioned in recipe titles—England, France, Germany, Ireland, Italy, Norway, Scotland, and Westphalia. Although we were a nation of immigrants, we were primarily from northern European countries and, even more specifically, the British Isles, whose cuisine tends to dominate here, reflecting the ancestry of most immigrants. It is clear, however, that French cooking was highly esteemed (a reflection of the nineteenth-century middle-class emulation of the upper-class preoccupation with French culture [McIntosh, 1995]), since several recipes and culinary terms given here are French.

The remarkable diversity of these "receipts" is also owing to the fact that the readers were rural women (albeit primarily from the middle class) because the nation during the Civil War period was primarily rural. A rural life implies that most of the meat consumed by the family came from animals killed on the premises. Of necessity, the cook had to use as much of the animal for meat as she could—sweetbreads were not a luxury, and tongues, brains, and feet had to be cooked well and served nicely. The master of the house (or sometimes the neighbors) also contributed to the table by hunting and fishing. There was, of course, a great abundance of game readily available in rural America, and this accounts for the large number of fish and game recipes. Overall, the meat diet was far more varied in the nineteenth century than it is today. The many recipes for fish and seafood testify to their abundance in the waters off the coasts and in rivers and streams.

The country cook was also a frugal cook, particularly when the nation was at war, and this explains not only the dishes for various animal parts but also the good number of recipes for leftovers and for seasonal produce; for example, several desserts were made with fresh fruits. That Hale's readers during the war years were not particularly wealthy is also suggested by the fact that, although cast-iron cooking ovens were introduced before 1830, she assumed her readers used a fireplace rather than a stove, for a spit and a hob are referred to in the roasting of poultry, for example.

Salads, as we know them, seem to have been relatively foreign to the palates of Hale's readers, for they do not commonly appear in the recipe column until the late decades of the century (the exceptions here are chicken salad and lobster salad). Gravies (broths) and sauces were very popular and were added to most meat dishes, soups, and even some fish dishes. Lemons also seem to have been in favor; their juice, rind, and gratings were all used. Cayenne pepper was popular, and unusual herbs and spices were frequently added to recipes, as were wines or other alcoholic beverages, often functioning as tenderizers or preservatives. The culinary trivia buff might note that, according to some sources, potato chips were invented by a chef in Saratoga, New York, in the 1880s (and called "Saratoga chips"), but a recipe for potato chips appeared in *Godey's* in 1865. Also, the terms "canapes" and "cottage pudding" may have appeared in print for the first time in the pages of *Godey's*.

The work involved in some of these recipes appalls those of us used to frozen foods and microwave ovens. The "Christening Cake," for example, calls for the cook to separate sixteen eggs, whisk the whites (perhaps with a pine whisk) to a complete froth, beat the yolks a full ten minutes by hand (perhaps with a three-pronged fork), and then beat the whole cake mixture for half an hour or longer. We have reproduced these recipes in their original form rather than adapting them for today's kitchens, in part to preserve them as social documents but also to provide the reader with the original recipe should he or she choose to follow it exactly, as well as to preserve the colorful and descriptive language: "Roll it up in the manner of a collared eel," "Take some grated toast and strew over it," "Suffer a few drops of vinegar to moisten them." Of course, in modern recipes the quantities of ingredients are usually given in volumes, not in weights as here. For the convenience of those who would like to try the recipes, an equivalent guide to proportions and weights is provided, and a glossary of less familiar ingredients and procedures can be found at the back of the book.

A good description of the cookware stocked in a typical middle-class American kitchen during the Civil War period can be found in Ellen M. Plante's *The American Kitchen* (1995). Plante notes that cookware was usually cast iron or tin and that copper pots and pans were expensive and therefore found only in the homes of the well-to-do. The following list of items was typical for the American kitchen in the period 1840-1869:

> *Large pots and pans:* long, oval fish kettle (as a preserve kettle); at least four saucepans of various sizes; several skillets; waffle iron; bread pans; toasting iron; tea kettle

> *Small tin items:* cake pans; pie pans; oil can; candle box; funnel; egg boiler; scoops; dippers; colander; bread boxes and cake boxes

> *Woodenware:* breadboard; spice boxes; salt box

> *Earthenware jars* with lids for butter, salt, and pickles

> *Baskets* of various sizes for gathering fruit, vegetables, and eggs. [Plante 1995: 51-52]

In selecting the recipes for this volume, we sought to provide a wide sampling from the magazine during the Civil War period, but at the same time we made a special effort to include recipes that would fall into the categories usually found in the cookbooks of today. Some sections may be underrepresented or perhaps even nonexistent here (e.g., shellfish or salad recipes) because of the scarcity of such recipes in the magazine.

Much of the terminology in the recipes differs from modern usage. Puddings were not necessarily puddings as we know them but were tied up in a "cloth pudding bag" and either boiled or steamed for many hours. They were a very common dessert, as were the many custards, creams, and fruit desserts, especially apples, which must have been the most plentiful of fruits and probably kept the best. "Tarts" were what we usually call "pies" and were often baked in a crock with only a pastry lid. It seems to have been customary during the nineteenth century to have several desserts in one menu. "Biscuit" refers to what we call a "cookie," and this volume contains one of the first uses of this word in its American sense. The term "cake" was used interchangeably for breads and cookies. The word "gravy," so frequently used, usually meant stock.

The dates in brackets mark the year the recipe appeared in *Godey's*. The footnotes are our editorial comments. A few of the illustrations are from *Godey's;* the remainder are from contemporary sources.

In compiling and editing these recipes, we aimed at more than providing a historical curiosity piece. All of these recipes are worth preserving in their own right, and many deserve to be used by twentieth-century cooks. Needless to say, we have used many ourselves. Some recipes we recognize as dishes our grandparents or great-grandparents, nineteenth-century immigrants from England, made on their Vermont farms in the 1920s and which we had all but forgotten. Although a few might turn a weak stomach, others are mouth-watering (such as Lemon Cheesecake, Madeira Cream Pudding, Lobster Salad, Beef Podovies, or even Sinee Kabaub, which is an earlier version of our Shish Kebab). Naturally the task of selecting and eliminating was most difficult because every one seemed to hold some point of interest and wonder. Yet we believe we have included not just those that will prove to be fascinating reading to those interested in the home front during the war years but also those that can be used today with delightful results—thanks to Godey and Hale.

THE BATTLE FRONT

Although *Godey's* had a very high circulation during the Civil War, the magazine's pages never included editorials or discussion of the war, for it was assumed that politics and social questions were not suitable for female readers. Indeed, if one read only *Godey's* for information on this period, one would never be aware of the bloody conflict raging outside the covers of the magazine. There were only two small exceptions. One letter to the editor alludes to the jobs that will be available to women after the war (because so many men will have died): "Many of the occupations which have heretofore been monopolized by men, but which are suited much better to the strength and ability of women, will be open to women. Work of all sorts will be necessary and *fashionable*" (January 1863: 93). In a later issue, about the time of Lee's surrender, Godey noted that subscription clubs had been received from the Union Army, and he commends the army for being refined and well behaved (March 1865: 284).

As in any war, life during the Civil War was difficult for the men and their families on both sides. Supplies of food were often limited, and the quality of foods that could be had was often poor. Needless to say, these shortages affected cooking and eating on both the battle front and the home front.

Food shortages were much more acute in the South than in the North, in part because of the blockade of southern ports that was ordered by President Abraham Lincoln just four days after the fall of Fort Sumter and remained in effect for the duration of the war. In addition, the South, although an agricultural region, was unable to organize its transportation system effectively enough to move food supplies quickly from storage areas to places where they were needed. The industrialized North not only had a more effective transportation system but could also make good use of its infant canning industry so that perishable items could be kept for many months. For example, the Union commandeered the entire output of Gail Borden's new condensed milk factory (Root and de Rochement, 1976). As the war continued, large agricultural areas in the South were destroyed by Northern troops. Consequently, the cost of food rose dramatically. In 1864, for example, while potatoes were selling for $2.25 a bushel in the North, they cost $25 a bushel in Richmond.

Confederate forces were frequently without adequate food supplies, and one source noted that food was often the prize of battle: "The inability of the [Confederate] government to furnish supplies forced the men to depend largely upon their own energy and ingenuity to obtain them. . . . The Confederate soldier relied greatly upon the abundant supplies of eatables which the enemy was kind enough to bring him, and he cheerfully risked his life for . . . what he called a 'square meal' " (McCarthy, 1882: 63-64). Food certainly was a determining factor in the outcome of the war. When Robert E. Lee surrendered to Ulysses S. Grant, he reported that his men had been without food for two days and asked Grant to supply his men with provisions. Lee's forces reportedly sent up a rousing cheer at the sight of the wagons of food that Grant provided.

Although on paper, rations were varied and sufficient, in actual fact this was almost never the case. For the most part rations consisted of corn bread and bad beef, with corn bread being the most constant. Supplies of vegetables, salt, and coffee were often short. But beef was also scarce or, more likely, rotten, so that in 1861 the commissary general recommended that rice and molasses be used as an occasional meat substitute (Moore, 1996), and mule meat was issued as standard ration in 1863 (Wiley, 1943). There are many reports of men existing for days on handfuls of parched corn or field peas. In addition to food shortages, the Confederate troops also frequently lacked adequate cooking ware and eating utensils (Wiley, 1943).

Poor food supplies led to the creation of new dishes. One dish, known as "cush" or "slosh," was made by putting small pieces of beef in bacon grease, then pouring in water and "stewing it." Next corn bread was crumbled in it, and the mixture was "stewed" again until all the water was cooked out. Another "stew" was made from Irish potatoes and green apples boiled together and then mashed and seasoned with salt, pepper, onions, or garlic. A third recipe called for making the batter for flapjacks and dropping it a spoonful at a time onto a stew of potatoes and meat. The whole was then stirred together in the kettle and next morning "we got meat, bread, and potatoes all in the same slice." Yet another dish known as "slapjack" consisted of a thick mixture of cornmeal or flour fried in a half-pan of bacon grease until the underside was brown, then flipped over to cook the top (Wiley, 1943).

Rations for the Union army, although hardly luxurious, appear to have been adequate. John Billings, a Grand Army of the Republic veteran, reported the following on the list of rations: salt pork, fresh beef, salt beef, ham or bacon (rare), hard bread (hardtack), soft bread, potatoes, onions (occasionally), flour, beans, split peas, rice, dried apples, dried peaches, desiccated vegetables, coffee, tea, sugar, molasses, vinegar, salt, and pepper.

According to Billings's *Hardtack and Coffee* (1887), a single day's rations for one Union soldier included 12 oz. pork or bacon, or 1 lb. 4 oz. salted beef (called "salt horse," this was often yellow-green in color and very unpalatable), or 1 lb. 4 oz. fresh beef, and 1 lb. 6 oz. soft bread or flour, or 1 lb. hard bread (hardtack), or 1 lb. 4 oz. corn meal.

For every 100 men, there were also distributed the following: 1 peck beans or peas (approx. 15 lbs.), 10 lbs. rice or hominy, 10 lbs. green coffee, or 8 lbs.

roasted and ground coffee (for a while a mixture of extract of coffee mixed with milk and sugar was issued), or 1 lb. 8 oz. tea (very rare), 15 lbs. sugar, 2 qts. salt, 4 qts. vinegar, 4 oz. pepper, 1/2 bushel of potatoes, 1 qt. molasses.

Whiskey was sometimes rationed out as the occasion arose. This occurred infrequently, but when it did, each man received one gill per day.

Billings adds that "vegetables, dried fruits, pickles, and pickled cabbage were occasionally issued to prevent scurvy, but in small quantities." According to another source, from the Sixteenth Vermont Volunteers, every meal was the same—beans and pork, three times a day!

Potatoes, when served, were generally boiled. Onions, when they were available, were fried. And split peas were cooked with pork. The unpopular "desiccated vegetables" were called "desecrated vegetables." These consisted of layers of cabbage leaves, turnip tops, sliced carrots, turnips, parsnips, and a few onions, which were dehydrated in large blocks (probably in ovens or kilns) and then cut into one-ounce servings (a cube of two or three inches) for each man. Issued to prevent scurvy, they were either made into soup or fried.

Bell I. Wiley (1952) reports that Union rations were more generous than those provided for the armies of England, France, Prussia, Austria, or Russia. At one point an increase in rations was revoked by Congress because it was believed to encourage waste. Wiley points out, however, that such rations did not mean that everyone was well fed all the time. Every regiment, particularly those in the West, suffered instances of great hunger.

Since each man was frequently responsible for his own meal, various methods developed for preparing the rations. Billings (1887) mentions several ways of eating hardtack (a term that he maintains originated during the Civil War among the men in the western armies): crumbled up in coffee, crumbled up in soup, eaten with raw salt pork as a sandwich, toasted before the fire and then buttered, or in "skillygalee," which is British slang for "thin broth" and was made by soaking hardtack in cold water, then frying it in pork fat until brown and salting to taste (a very indigestible dish according to Billings).

Other "recipes" from the army included the following:

Ashcakes. Cornmeal mixed with salt and water; wrapped in cabbage leaves and cooked in ashes until firm.

Baked beans. Usually cooked with pork, but sometimes baked in a kettle placed in a hole in the ground and then covered and banked with hot coals and allowed to cook overnight.

Hardtack pudding. Hardtack pounded into a powder, mixed with water and flour if available, then kneaded into a dough, rolled out like a piecrust, and filled with apples or anything available. Finally it would be wrapped up in a cloth and boiled for an hour.

Hell-fire stew. Hardtack boiled in water and bacon grease.

Lobscouse. A nautical term for a stew of pieces of meat, vegetables, and hardtack.

Milk toast. Hardtack soaked in condensed milk.

Coffee was the beverage of the soldier simply because tea was less available. He was issued a ration of it and frequently mixed his ground coffee together with his ration of sugar, then boiled the mixture together, adding some condensed milk before drinking it. The nation as a whole still preferred tea, but probably the availability of coffee as a ration increased its acceptance after the war. In 1862 only three pounds of coffee were used nationwide to every seven pounds of tea, but by 1885, nine pounds of coffee were used for every one pound of tea.

THE HOME FRONT

The mid-nineteenth century marked a transition between a time when households made or grew almost all their own products and foods to a time when these were supplied commercially. New factories were being built, and consumers now had some products that were standardized nationally rather than custom-made locally. As a result of this industrialization, many new products had been developed during the early part of the nineteenth century, making life easier for those at home. Kathleen Smallzried in *The Everlasting Pleasure* (1956) summarized the changes that had occurred by

1830: commercial soap was available, dairy products could be purchased rather than being made at home (bottled milk was sold in New York in the 1850s), commercially butchered and cured meats could be found at the store, the icebox was sold commercially, and the wood or coal range was available for cooking, replacing the fireplace. (Although the iron range or stove was available by the 1830s, its adoption by the general public was very slow; many people simply could not afford such stoves, and they were not in wide use until after the Civil War.) In 1848 the hand-cranked ice cream freezer was patented, and many washing machines had been patented by 1850.

The Mason jar, perfected in 1859, helped spur the development of commercial canning, even though home canning did not become widespread until the development of the pressure cooker in 1874. The war contributed to the canning industry because of the need to feed soldiers. Canned condensed milk was popular among Union army recruits, and other canned goods were also available (although not always in the army), including various fruits, meat, oysters, green peas and other vegetables, sardines, salmon, and even lobster.

Major changes had also occurred to help those who baked at home, which was almost everyone. One of the great burdens in making cakes, for example, was that to get them light enough required beating the batter for literally hours at times (see, for example, the recipe in this volume for Christening Cake). In the 1790s pearlash (potassium carbonate) had been discovered as a means to make dough rise. Its use gradually declined after 1840, when saleratus, or baking soda, was introduced, which functioned more effectively but which required the addition of sour milk or cream of tartar to

 make it work. Then an enterprising individual decided to combine baking soda with cream of tartar and sell the product commercially. The result, called baking powder, was introduced in 1856 and saved hours of beating eggs or batter.

Yeast, an even better product, became commercially available around 1868, although other versions could be made at home before that time and frequently were. In fact, *Godey's* recipe column often included recipes for yeast; in 1863 alone, the column included directions for making peach leaf yeast, potato yeast, and hop beer yeast.

The recipes in *Godey's* do not necessarily follow these historical milestones, however. Although stoves were available, many of the recipes assume the cook is using a fireplace. There are recipes that appeared in the 1860s after baking powder was available but that do not add leavening agents at all and that call for beating the batter for long periods of time. There are many recipes that call for yeast. And there are recipes that appeared after commercial yeast was available but call for saleratus and a recipe in 1862 that called for baking soda and cream of tartar. How can we account for these various uses and dates? One possibility is that in a period when technical advances were being made more rapidly than before, not all recipes would necessarily have been changed to accommodate the newest technical advances. Another possibility is that since these recipes were often contributed by readers, there would be a wide range in the technical expertise of the contributors. A recipe that had been in one's family for a generation or two, for example, is likely to be repeated in a similar form, rather than "modernized" with new products and technical advances. And, perhaps most likely, some rural cooks simply did not have access to newer products until many years after their introduction.

Oatmeal does not appear in these pages, nor does it appear in the list of rations for the Union soldier. When oatmeal appears in *Godey's* during these years, it is primarily as a food for infants or invalids. It is thought that it did not gain favor as a breakfast food in America until the late 1860s or 1870s. Its popularity is sometimes attributed to Queen Victoria, who recommended it after a trip to Scotland when she saw the ruddy complexions of Scottish children and attributed their good health to the consumption of oatmeal.

Throughout the country various fruits were just beginning to become popular in the mid-nineteenth century. Oranges were available but expensive. They were usually imported, and it was not until they began to be grown in Florida and California in the late 1800s that they became more accessible to the average middle American. This volume, however, includes several recipes containing oranges, such as Orange Pudding and Salade d'Oranges. Grapefruit, which originated in Jamaica, had not yet entered the American consciousness to any great extent, and bananas did not become popular until after they were exhibited in Philadelphia in 1876 (Rorabaugh, 1987). Coconuts and pineapples began arriving from Cuba by the 1850s and could be had occasionally, as evidenced by their presence in these pages. Lemons were a favorite for flavoring, especially lemon peel (or zest). Apples, of course, were home-grown and plentiful in the North. As a consequence, they are used in many dishes and (sometimes in dried versions) in all seasons. Berries, grapes, and watermelon could be grown locally and are all present here.

The reader will notice very few recipes containing chocolate. As a hot beverage, chocolate had been present in the American colonies since 1765, but eating chocolate was not manufactured until 1847 and then in England. Milk chocolate was developed in Switzerland in 1876, when dried milk was added. Before the end of the century, chocolate squares would become a common ingredient in baking, but during the Civil War era they were unknown.

Before the common use of oatmeal, breakfast on a small New England farm in the 1860s—served after the farmer had already done many chores—was typically cornmeal mush with cream; sometimes a little maple syrup was added as a sweetener. At the same table there may also have been corn dodgers (cornmeal griddle cakes), tea, and doughnuts made from wheat flour ground locally. Dinner, of course, was the large meal in the middle of the day and might consist of boiled potatoes and ham, fresh pork, or perhaps corned beef. There would always be pie—apple in the winter, rhubarb in the spring, and a berry in the summer and fall. Mincemeat pie (perhaps made with boiled cider and venison) could be served at any time but probably was more often seen in the fall and winter months (see Mussey, 1965). A Saturday dinner would commonly be boiled salted codfish; leftovers would be eaten the next morning. A customary Sunday dinner consisted of baked beans, brown bread, and Indian pudding. In the evening the Yankee family sat down to supper, a much lighter meal than dinner, perhaps as little as johnnycake and milk, or bread and milk with maple syrup, or flapjacks sprinkled with brown sugar, followed by a custard.

Meals in the rural South were just as plain as those in the North. "Hog 'n hominy" (pork and boiled corn) was standard fare. An inn in South Carolina in 1861 served hog and hominy and corn cake for breakfast; waffles and hog and hominy for dinner; and hog and hominy and corn cake for supper (McCutcheon, 1993). A traveler in Mississippi before the Civil War reported on his meal with a rural pioneer household: "The husband came in from hunting with his deer. The wife took half a gallon of white corn meal, poured boiling water on it, added salt, and shaped it into small pones, which she wrapped in fresh shucks of corn and then laid them in the fireplace under a bed of hot ashes. Supper was thus broiled venison and hot ashcakes. The same ingredients of the ashcake, if spread thinly on a hoe or iron sheet and cooked in the open air, would be called hoecake. And the same cooked in an oven would be called pone" (Phillips, 1929: 349).

Staples for cooking in the South included pork, cornmeal (usually white, not yellow as was preferred in the North), and sweet potatoes. "Meals almost always included some form of pork, cornbread, and sour milk. Sometimes wild game, beef, chicken, sweet potatoes, field peas, rice and greens either substituted for or supplemented the usual fare" (McWhiney, 1988: 81). The South did not have the large numbers of dairy herds that were seen in the North, and milk was not as available or as popular as in the North. The poorer classes drank water or water mixed with molasses. Apples did not grow well in the South, but peaches did, so the peach became to the South what the apple was to the North. Besides the ubiquitous corn, other important vegetables in the southern fare included beans, cowpeas, rice, and turnips. Pork was available because of the large number of razorback hogs that were often allowed to roam freely and to forage for themselves in the woods or in town.

During the war, however, the southern home front as well as its army suffered from sometimes severe food shortages. Owners of large plantations, who were used to giving balls and dinner parties with an abundance of delicious foods and drinks, were forced into feeding their families anything that was available and edible. A Georgia's family's food situation during the summer of

1865 was grim: "We have no kind of meat in our house but ham and bacon, and have to eat hominy instead of rice at dinner. . . . Cornfield peas have been our staple diet for the last ten days. Mother has cooked them in every variety of style she ever heard of, but they are cornfield peas still. All this would have been horribly mortifying a year or two ago, but everyone knows how it is now, and I am glad to have even cornfield peas to share with the soldiers" (Andrews, 1995: 302). Another Confederate woman wrote in her diary about the high cost of food at Christmas 1862: "To form some idea of the extravagant prices of things . . . I will mention that the apples for the dessert were 10 cts. a piece, the oranges 30 and 40 cts., the icing of a pound cake, $1.50. . . . The baked and boiled turkey would alone have cost 8 dollars" (Burr, 1990).

Food shortages forced residents on the southern home front to make substitutions for products that had been easily accessible before the war. The North, in contrast, had enough food to be able to export the surplus to Europe (Burroughs, 1992). Since *Godey's* was published in the North, there are no recipes in the present volume that reflect the great privations of the South or any of these substitutions, but, because there are southern recipes in this volume, we thought it would be instructive to note the substitutions the southern cook might have used in preparing them. (For some actual southern recipes that make use of substitutions, see *The Confederate Receipt Book* [1960] and Burroughs [1992]).

Butter: The South did not have the dairy products available in the North, so pork lard (or bacon grease) was frequently substituted for butter (Burroughs, 1992). When animal fats became scarce, sunflower seed oil was used (Hooker, 1981).

Hot chocolate: One southern woman reported that during the war chocolate was unavailable so a substitute for hot chocolate was invented from peanuts. The peanuts were roasted, skinned, and pounded in a mortar. The result when blended with boiled milk and sugar was found "delightful to our palates" (Clay-Clopton, 1905).

Coffee: Coffee was coming into popular use during this period, and its shortage caused considerable discomfort among coffee drinkers. A wide variety of substitutes was used: parched and ground acorns, beans, chicory, corn, cottonseed, dandelion roots, groundnuts, okra seed, peanuts, peas, parched rice, rye, sweet potato, and wheat (Hooker, 1981; Porcher, 1863).

Hops: Hops were the major ingredient in yeast manufacture but were not available in the South. The herb "life everlasting" and artichoke leaves were used in place of hops (Burroughs, 1992; Porcher, 1863).

Meat: Obviously meat was in great demand, and shortages occurred in both armies as well as on the southern home front. When hunting could be done, wild game could supply the demand, but southerners who were starved for meat sometimes consumed mules, dogs, cats, rats, and other "unusual" sources of protein (Hooker, 1981). Frances Porcher (1863) recommends the use of groundnuts as a meat substitute.

Molasses: Porcher (1863) suggests watermelon syrup as a good substitute for molasses.

Saleratus: Saleratus was manufactured in the North and, therefore, not readily available in the South. A substitute for saleratus was lye or potash, which acted as a leavening agent (Burroughs, 1992).

Sugar: Sugar became especially scarce after the Union army occupied southern Louisiana. The main substitute for sugar was sorghum, but other substitutes could be used—honey, maple sugar, boiled sap from butternut or walnut trees, sugar beets, and persimmons (Hooker, 1981).

Tea: Herb teas were used when black tea was not available. The more common of these were the leaves of the black alder, blackberry, currant, holly, huckleberry, and raspberry bushes and the bark of the sassafras tree (Hooker 1981; Porcher, 1863). Confederate soldiers made "tea" from corn bran, ginger, or various herbs (Wiley, 1943).

Vanilla: The leaves of the peach tree were used as a replacement for vanilla (Porcher, 1863).

Vegetables: When vegetables became scarce in the cities, herbs and flowers were eaten. Hooker (1981) reports that in 1863 the only fresh vegetable available in Richmond markets was watercress.

Wheat flour: Substitutes included cornmeal and rice flour (Burroughs, 1992). Seeds from the white beech, as well as ground doura corn, are recommended by Porcher (1863).

Because we use only recipes that were printed in the magazine during the decade of the 1860s, some traditional favorites are not included. For example, some

Yankee dishes that are absent but that were in fact popular include fish chowder and clam chowder, Boston baked beans, and chicken pie. Examples of popular southern dishes well known at the time but not included here are catfish, possum, fried chicken, molasses custard, and huckleberry pie. Nonetheless, both sides of the Mason-Dixon line are represented. Some specific examples of traditional Yankee fare in these pages are Brown Bread, Indian Pudding, Plum Pudding, Mincemeat, Boston Cream Cakes, and Vermont Currant Cake. Representatives from below the Mason-Dixon line include Hominy, Pone, Okra Soup, Chicken Gumbo, South Carolina Johnny Cake, Pillau, and Sweet Potato Pudding. We hope you enjoy reading and perhaps sampling these and the other recipes as much as we have. We might add that the majority of recipes are seeing print for the first time in well over a century.

GUIDE TO EQUIVALENTS AND SUBSTITUTIONS

Allspice, ground	5 tablespoons	1 ounce
Almonds,		
In shell	3½ pounds	1 pound shelled
Blanched, whole	1 cup	5½ ounces
Blanched, slivered	1 cup	4 ounces

Unblanched, whole	1 cup	6 ounces
Unblanched, ground	2⅔ cups	1 pound
Unblanched, slivered	5⅔ cups	1 pound

Anchovies   1 cup   8 ounces

Apples   3 cups, pared, sliced   1 pound, unpared
3½ to 4 pounds raw   1 pound, dried
About 10 apples   1 pound, dried

Applesauce   2 cups   1 pound

Apricots, dried   3¼ cup   1 pound
Fresh   5½ pounds   1 pound dried
Cooked and drained   3 cups   1 pound

Arrowroot, thickener   1½ teaspoons   1 tablespoon flour

2 teaspoons   1 tablespoon cornstarch

Baking powder   1 teaspoon   ¼ teaspoon baking soda plus ⅝ teaspoon cream of tartar

Double acting   1 teaspoon   1½ teaspoons phosphate or tartrate baking powder

Bay leaf   ¼ teaspoon, crushed   1 whole bay leaf

Beans, dried   6 cups cooked   1 pound or 2½ cups

Beans, green, fresh   2½ cups cooked   1 pound or 3 cups

Bread crumbs, dry   ¼ cup   1 slice bread
    Coarse, day-old   9 cups   1 pound
    Coarse, day-old   1 cup   1¾ ounces
    Dried, sieved   4 cups   1 pound
    Soft   ½ cup   1 slice bread

Butter, 1 stick   8 tablespoons = ½ cup   4 ounces
                2 tablespoons   1 ounce
      1 cup   1 cup margarine   8 ounces
                1 cup vegetable fat
                ⅞ cup of lard
                ¾ cup + 1 tablespoon clarified bacon fat
                ⅔ cup clarified chicken fat
                ½ cup of suet
      1 quart   1 pound

Cabbage   ½ pound minced   3 cups packed
                1 pound, about 1 head   4½ cups
                                        shredded

Carrots, fresh   3 cups shredded or
                2½ cups diced   1 pound

Cauliflower, florets   2 cups   1 pound

Celery seed   4 tablespoons   1 ounce

Cheese, cottage   1 cup   ½ pound

Cheese, dry   4 cups   1 pound
    Freshly shredded   1 cup   ¼ pound

Chocolate   8 ounces melted   1 cup

Chocolate, unsweetened 1 square   1 ounce
    4 tablespoons grated   1 ounce
    3 tablespoons cocoa plus
    1 tablespoon butter or fat   1 ounce

Cinnamon, ground   4 tablespoons   1 ounce

Cloves, ground   5 tablespoons   1 ounce
    Whole   1 cup   3 ounces

Cocoa   4 cups   1 pound
            ¼ cup   1 ounce
            3 tablespoons + 1 tablespoon
            butter or fat   1 ounce
                                unsweetened chocolate

Coconut
    Unsweetened, shredded 5 cups   1 pound
    Sweetened, shredded   4 cups   1 pound
    Dried, chopped   1 tablespoon 1⅓ tablespoon
                                       fresh
    Flaked   1⅓ cups   3½ ounces
    Grated   1 cup   1⅓ cups
                                       flaked
    Whole, average size   2 cups chopped

Coffee   40-50 6-ounce cups   1 pound
    Regular   5-5½ cups   1 pound
    Instant   1 cup   2 ounces

Cornmeal/Indian meal 3 cups   1 pound
                          1 cup uncooked 4-4½ cups
                                          cooked

Cornstarch   3 cups   1 pound
For thickening, substitute 1 tablespoon cornstarch for:
                          2 tablespoons flour,
                          5 teaspoons rice flour,
                          2 teaspoons arrowroot

Cracker crumbs   8 cups   1 pound
                          1 cup   2 ounces
                          4 tablespoons ½ ounce

Cranberries, raw   4 cups   1 pound
    Sauce   2 cups   1 pound

Cream of tartar   3 tablespoons 1 ounce

Currants, dried   3 cups   1 pound

Curry powder   4 tablespoons 1 ounce

Eggs, extra large	4	about 1 cup
Large	5	about 1 cup
Medium	6	about 1 cup
Small	7	about 1 cup
Egg whites, extra large	6	about 1 cup
Large	8	about 1 cup
Medium	10-11	about 1 cup
Small	11-12	about 1 cup
Egg yolks, extra large	10-11	about 1 cup
Large (2 ounces)	12	about 1 cup
Medium	13-14	about 1 cup
Small	15-16	about 1 cup
Figs, dried	2⅔ cups chopped	1 pound

Flour

Bread and all purpose	4 cups (1 quart)	1 pound
Cake	4½ cups	1 pound
Graham, unsifted	3½ cups	1 pound
Bran, unsifted	4 cups	½ pound
Rice flour	3 cups	1 pound

*Substitute 1 cup minus 2 tablespoons for
1 cup of all-purpose flour*

Garlic	1 small clove	⅛ teaspoon powder
Gelatin, granulated	¼ cup	1 ounce
	1 tablespoon	¼ ounce

*1 tablespoon will solidify
2 cups liquid*

Ginger
candied, washed of sugar,
or 1 tablespoon raw ½ teaspoon powdered

Ginger
green root, (race) 1 inch square ¼ teaspoon ground

Ginger, ground	4 tablespoons	1 ounce
6 teaspoons or 2 tablespoons		½ ounce

Glacé fruits 3 teaspoons or 1 tablespoon ⅓ ounce

Hominy, raw 1 cup   6 ounces

Honey 1 cup   1¼ cups sugar plus ¼ cup liquid

Horseradish
    grated 1 tablespoon   2 tablespoons bottled

Lard 2 cups   1 pound

Lemons 1   1-3 tablespoons juice
    1 teaspoon juice ½ teaspoon vinegar
    1 teaspoon grated rind   ½ teaspoon
            lemon extract
    3 tablespoons grated rind   ½ ounce

Macaroni, uncooked 4 cups 1 pound
    1 cup uncooked 2¼ cups cooked

Meat, diced, cooked 2 cups 1 pound
    Chopped, raw 2 cups 1 pound

Milk, whole 1 cup 1 cup water plus
                  1½ teaspoons butter
    1 quart 1 quart skim plus
                  3 tablespoons cream

Milk, sour 1 cup 1 tablespoon vinegar
                  or lemon juice to
                  1 cup of milk.
                  Let stand 5 minutes.

Molasses 1½ cups 1 pound

Mushrooms
    Fresh, whole 3 cups 8 ounces or 1 cup
                  sliced, cooked
    Canned 6 ounces drained ½ pound fresh
    Dried 3 ounces 1 pound fresh

Mustard
    Dry or powdered 1 teaspoon 1 tablespoon, prepared
    Prepared 1 tablespoon 1 ounce

Mustard, seed 3 tablespoons · 1 ounce

Nuts *(see also almonds)*

    Pecans 2½ pounds in shell · 1 pound shelled, 4½ cups

    Walnuts 2-2½ pounds in shell · 1 pound shelled, 4½ cups of halves

    5½ cups, ground · 1 pound

Nutmeg 1 whole, grated · about 2-3 teaspoons

Oats, rolled 5 cups · 1 pound

    Fine 4 cups · 1 pound

Onions

    Chopped 3 cups · 1 pound

    Grated 4 tablespoons · 3 ounces

Oranges 1 medium · 6-8 tablespoons juice

    1 medium · ¾ cup diced

    1 medium, rind grated · 2-3 tablespoons

Oysters, shucked 2¼ cups · 1 pound

Peaches, medium sized 4 · 1 pound or 2 cups, sliced

Pears, medium sized 4 · 1 pound or 2 cups, sliced

Peas, frozen 3 cups · 1 pound

    Split 2⅓ cups · 1 pound

Peel, candied, citron 1 cup · 3 ounces

    Candied fruit 3 cups · 1 pound

Potatoes, raw 3 medium · 1 pound

    Raw, sliced 2½ cups · 1 pound

    Mashed 1 cup · 7 ounces

    Cooked, diced 2¼ cups · 1 pound

Potatoes, sweet, raw 3 medium · 1 pound

    Raw, sliced 2½ cups · 1 pound

    Cooked 1 cup · 8 ounces

Pumpkin, cooked	2½ cups	1 pound
Raisins, seeded, whole	3¼ cups	1 pound
Seedless, whole	2¾ cups	1 pound
Rhubarb (pieplant)		
Raw, in pieces	2¼ cups	1 pound
Cooked	2 cups	1 pound
Rice, uncooked	1 cup	7 ounces
Ground	1 cup	6 ounces
Uncooked	2 cups (1 pound)	6 cups cooked
Precooked, dehydrated	2 cups	2⅔ cups cooked
Salmon, canned	2 cups	1 pound
Fresh, flaked	3 cups	1 pound
Salt	2 tablespoons	1 ounce
	1 teaspoon	.167 ounce
	2 teaspoons	.33 ounce
	1 salt spoon	⅛ teaspoon
Shortening, melted	1 cup	7 ounces
Solid	2 cups	1 pound
Shrimp	3¼ cups	1 pound
Soda (baking)	7 teaspoons	1 ounce
Spaghetti, raw, broken	4 cups	1 pound
2-inch pieces	1 cup dry	about 1¾ cups cooked
12-inch pieces	1 pound dry	about 6½ cups cooked
Spinach, freshly cooked	2½ cups	1 pound
Strawberries, fresh, whole	1 quart	4 cups sliced
Suet	2 cups	1 pound
	1 cup	8 ounces
Chopped	½ cup	4 ounces

Sugar, brown

Packed loosely	3 cups	1 pound
Packed firmly	2¼ cups	1 pound
Packed firmly	1 cup	1 cup of granulated

Sugar, granulated

	2 cups	1 pound
Fruit (super-fine)	3½ cups	1 pound
Confectioners'	3½-4 cups (1 quart)	1 pound
Confectioners'	1¾ cups	1 cup of granulated
Loaf	1 quart	1 pound

Tapioca, minute 2½ cups 1 pound

Minute, for thickening 1 tablespoon 1 tablespoon flour

Minute, for thickening 1 tablespoon 1 tablespoon cornstarch

Minute, for thickening 1½ tablespoons equals ¼ cup of pearl, soaked for at least one hour

Tea, dry 6 cups 1 pound (makes 125 cups)

Tomatoes

fresh, peeled, quartered 1 cup 5 ounces

1 cup packed ½ cup of tomato sauce plus ½ cup of water

Vinegar 2 cups 16 ounces

Water 2 cups 1 pound

Yeast, active, dry 1 package 1 tablespoon

Yeast, compressed 1 cake (3/5 ounce) 1 package dry yeast

Zests, fresh grated citrus rinds

To substitute

1 teaspoon freshly grated zest = 2 tablespoons fresh juice

1 teaspoon dried zest or ½ teaspoon extract or

2 teaspoons grated candied peel

Liquid Measures

1 dessert spoon equals	2 teaspoons
1 saltspoon equals	⅛ teaspoon
16 large tablespoonfuls equal	½ pint, 1 cup
8 large tablespoonfuls equal	1 gill, ½ cup
4 large tablespoonfuls equal	½ gill, ¼ cup
2 gills equal	½ pint, 1 cup
2 pints equal	1 quart, 4 cups
4 quarts equal	1 gallon, 16 cups
A common-sized tumbler holds	½ pint, 1 cup
A common-sized wine glass holds	½ gill, 4-6 fluid ounces
60 drops equal	1 teaspoon
4 noggins equal	1 pint
1 teacupful equals	4-6 fluid ounces
1 coffee cup equals	⅝ to 1 cup (varies)
1 pottle (an old measure) equals	½ gallon
1 fluid drachm (dram) equals	⅛ fluid ounce, ¾ teaspoon
Hogshead (of wine) is	a large cask, usual capacity of 63-140 gallons

Quantities of Meat, Poultry, and Fish to Buy

	TO SERVE 2	TO SERVE 4
Beef		
Chopped	¾ pound	1½ pounds
Dried	3 oz.	6 oz.
Liver	¾ pound	1½ pounds
Roast, pot (rump or round chuck, shoulder)	2½ pounds	3½-4 pounds
Roast, rolled rib	1 rib	2 ribs

	TO SERVE 2	TO SERVE 4
Roast, sirloin	3 pounds	3½-4 pounds
Roast, standing rib	1 rib	2 ribs
Steak, sirloin, porterhouse	½-¾ pound per person	
Steak, T-bone, club, rib, or tenderloin	½-¾ pound per person	

Lamb

	TO SERVE 2	TO SERVE 4
Breast (unboned)	2½-3 pounds	3½-4 pounds
Chops, loin or shoulder	2-3 chops	4-6 chops
Chops, rib	4 chops	8 chops
Cutlets or steaks	1-1¼ pounds	2-2½ pounds
Kidneys	4 kidneys	8 kidneys
Whole leg—16 servings	(Don't roast under 3 pounds)	

Pork

	TO SERVE 2	TO SERVE 4
Bacon	4 slices	8 slices
Butt, smoked, boneless shoulder	1-1½ pounds	2-2½ pounds
Chops, loin or shoulder	2-3 chops	4-6 chops
Ham, slice	1 pound	2 pounds
Loin roast	1½ pounds (4- 5 chops)	3 pounds
Liver	¾ pound	1½ pounds
Sausages	½ pound	1 pound

Veal

	TO SERVE 2	TO SERVE 4
Breast (unboned)	2-2½ pounds	3½-4 pounds
Cutlets or steak	1 pound	2 pounds
Chops, loin or rib	3-4 chops	6-8 chops
Loin	2 pound (4- 5 chops)	3½-4 pounds
Shoulder (unboned)	2½-3 pounds	4½-5 pounds
Kidneys	2 kidneys	4 kidneys

	TO SERVE 2	TO SERVE 4
Fish		
Fillets	¾ pound	1½ pounds
Steaks	1 pound	2 pounds
Whole	1½ pounds	3 pounds

Venison

A 6-pound boned shoulder serves 8
Roast—same as for beef

Poultry

Chicken fricassee	4½-5 pounds serves 6
Chicken, roast	¾-1 pound per person
Chicken, fried or broiled	½ or ¼ chicken per person depending on size
Duck, roast	¾-1 pound (drawn, per person)
Duck, mallard, roast	1½ pounds drawn weight serves 2
Duck, wild, roast	1-1½ pounds per person
Goose, roast	Allow 1-1¼ pounds drawn per person. 7 pounds serves 6.
Turkey, roast	Allow ¾ pound per person. 15 pounds serves 20.

Rabbit

Fried	2 rabbits, 1¼ pound each, serves 4
Stew	2½-3 pounds serves 6-8

Pigeons, quail, or partridges

Usually allow 1 per person

Partridge pie	3 partridges serves 6

Useful Information

Bouquet garni: A bundle of herbs to flavor stocks and stews. Bay leaf, thyme, and parsley are the usual ones, tied with string to a rib of celery or a leek. Sometimes a sprig of rosemary is included. This should be added during the last half hour of cooking. If fresh herbs are not available, you can make up ten to twelve small cheesecloth bags from the following mixture: 2 tablespoons dried parsley, 1 tablespoon each thyme and marjoram, 2 bay leaves, crumpled, and 2 tablespoons dried celery leaves.

Egg wash (or glaze): One egg yolk mixed with 1 or 2 tablespoons milk or water; can be sprinkled with granulated sugar.

Fruit syrup: Can be served with milk, yogurt, fresh fruits, white wine, mineral water, ice cream, pancakes, waffles, and other foods.

Oven temperatures:

Very low	250-275°
Low	300-325°
Moderate	350-375°
Hot oven	400-425°
Very hot	450-475°
Extremely hot	500-525°

Rose water and orange water: Because of the high cost of these flower waters, food economists today advise us to use them sparingly in amounts comparable to flavorings.

Salt brine for pickling: A 10 percent brine is about the strongest used in food processing today. It is made by dissolving 1½ cups of salt in 1 gallon of water or 6 tablespoons to a quart. You should allow 2 gallons of brine plus food enough to fill a 4-gallon container.

Simple syrup for fruit drinks: Combine 3 cups of sugar with 3 cups of water and bring to a boil. Stir until the sugar is dissolved. Cover and boil for 5 minutes without stirring. Cool. Store in refrigerator in a clean covered container. Makes about 4¼ cups of syrup.

Sweet herbs: Use equal parts of fresh parsley, tarragon, chives, and chervil, minced. If dried herbs are used, use only half the amounts. They are usually added the last few minutes of cooking. *Fines herbes* is a similar blend of herbs that can be purchased at your local supermarket.

Syrups for canning fruits:

Thin	About 5 cups:	2 cups sugar	4 cups water
Medium	About 5½ cups:	3 cups sugar	4 cups water
Heavy	About 6½ cups:	4¾ cups sugar	4 cups water

Stir until sugar is dissolved, then boil slowly about 5 minutes. Use boiling hot to fill jars of fruit for canning.

White sauces:

THIN	MEDIUM	THICK
1 tablespoons butter	2-3 tablespoons butter	4 tablespoons butter
1 tablespoon flour	2-3 tablespoons flour	4 tablespoons flour

CIVIL WAR RECIPES

THIN	MEDIUM	THICK
¼ teaspoon salt	¼ teaspoon salt	¼ teaspoon salt
⅛ teaspoon pepper	⅛ teaspoon pepper	⅛ teaspoon pepper
1 cup milk	1 cup milk	1 cup milk

Melt butter, stir in flour, add seasonings, blend well, gradually add milk, stirring constantly.

Yeast: 1 cake yeast (⅗ ounce) or 1 tablespoon dry (1 envelope) to 1½ cups liquid; ½ ounce of yeast raises 4 cups of flour in about 1 ½ to 2 hours. One ounce of yeast raises 28 cups of flour in about 7 hours.

BILLS OF FARE

The following bills of fare were selected from the many given in Godey's "as a guide to housekeepers in selecting dishes for the table".

Potatoes were always served, regardless of the season. Chicken was usually served in the summer, perhaps because on a small farm that was the most appropriate time for "culling" the flock. Dessert was typically a pudding, hence the large number of puddings included in this volume.

Those recipes preceded by a bullet (•) can be found in this volume.

JANUARY

• *Fish with Piquante Sauce*

• *Potatoes*   *Fried Jerusalem Artichokes*

Remove. —Sirloin of Beef [Beef Steak] or Fillet of Beef with Mushrooms

Pumpkin Pudding

Lemon Soufflé

FEBRUARY

• *Roast Turkey*

• *Mashed Potatoes*   *Fried Jerusalem Artichokes*

• *Fricassee of Cold Roast Beef*

• *Plum Pudding*

MARCH

French Maigre Soup

Remove. —Veal Cutlets, garnished with Bacon

• *Potatoes*   • *Roast Griskin [leg] of Pork*

Cauliflower au Gratin

Apple Souffle Pudding

• *Open German Tart*

APRIL

- Boiled [Roast] Leg of Mutton

- Potatoes · Broccoli

· Curry of Veal

· Fancy Puff [Boston Cream Cakes]

· Fruit Tart [Lemon Pie]

MAY

Rich Onion Soup

· Harricot of Veal

· Potatoes   Asparagus

· Ground Rice (Thun) Pudding

· Rhubarb Fool

JUNE

· Lamb Cutlets

· Potatoes   Asparagus

· Roast Veal Stuffed

Strawberry Soufflé

JULY

• *Broiled Lamb [Steak]*

• *Roast Ducks [Wild Ducks]*

Young Potatoes   *Peas*

• *Ground-Rice (Thin) Pudding*

Raspberry Cream

AUGUST

• *Boiled Ham*

• *Lamb Cutlets*

• *Potatoes*   • *Lettuce Peas*

Strawberry Soufflé

Stewed Currants

SEPTEMBER

Relishing Rashers of Bacon

• *Potatoes*   *Stewed Tomatoes*

• *Beef-Steak Pie*

• *A Delicate Pudding [Baked Custard]*

• *Apple Charlotte [Brown Charlotte Pudding]*

OCTOBER

• *A Cheap Green Pea Soup*

• *Remove. — Baked Mutton Chops*

• *Potatoes*   *Broad Beans*

• *Boeuf a la Ménagère*

• *Brace of Partridges [Partridge Pie]*   *Stewed Apples*

• *Apple Tartlets [Green Apple Pie]*   • *Custard*

NOVEMBER

• *Rabbit Curry*

• *Potatoes*   • *Fried Artichokes*

• *Maccaroni and Cheese*

• *Roast Leg of Pork*

• *Thun Pudding*

THANKSGIVING

• *Roast Turkey with Cranberry Sauce*

• *Turnips*

Boiled Fowls with Celery Sauce

• *Salsify [Vegetable Oyster Cakes]*

• *Boiled Ham*

• *Winter Squash*   • *[Hot] Cole-Slaw*

Stewed Goose

• *Sweet Potato Pudding*   • *Pumpkin Pudding*

Baked Lemon Pudding [Soufflé]

CHRISTMAS

Boiled Turkey with Oyster Sauce   *Beet Root*

Roast Goose with Applesauce   • *[Hot] Cole-Slaw*

• *Boiled Ham*   • *Turnips*

• *Winter Squash*   *Savory Chicken Pie*   • *Salsify Cakes*

• *Mince Pie*   • *Plum Pudding*   *Lemon Custard*   • *Cranberry Tart*

NEW YEAR'S DINNER

• *Mock Turtle Soup*

Roast Turkey with Cranberry Sauce

• *Stewed Celery*   *Pickled Beet Root*

Boiled Turkey with Celery Sauce

• *Winter Squash*   • *Snitz and Knep*   • *[Hot] Cole-Slaw*
[Ham and Apples]

• *Smoke — Tongue [Beef Tongue]*   • *Salsify*

• *A Curry of Meat [Curry of Veal]*

• *Plum Pudding*   • *Mince Pie*   *Orange Jelly*   • *Coffee Cream*

BEVERAGES

MILK LEMONADE*
[1861 AND 1862]

Dissolve six ounces of loaf-sugar in a pint of boiling water, and mix with them a quarter pint of lemon-juice, and the same quantity of sherry; then add three-quarters of a pint of cold milk, stir the whole well together, and pass it through a jelly-bag till clear.

* This is an unusual recipe but very tasty iced
or hot (like a toddy). For Civil War-era
recipes for lemonade and orangeade
(as well as recipes for alcoholic drinks)
see Johnson and Johnson (1992).

Barley Water
[1860]

One ounce of pearl barley, half an ounce of white sugar, and the rind of a lemon; put it into a jug. Pour upon it one quart of boiling water, and let it stand for eight or ten hours; then strain off the liquor, adding a slice of lemon, if desirable. This infusion makes a most delicious and nutritious beverage, and will be grateful to persons who cannot drink the horrid decoction usually given. It is an admirable basis for lemonade, negus* or weak punch, a glass of rum being the proportion for a quart.

* Negus is a drink made of wine, hot water, and lemon juice, sweetened and flavored with spices. It was named for its inventor, Col. Francis Negus (d. 1732). Negus was a popular drink in England during the 1700s.

Blackberry Syrup*
[1860]

Make a simple syrup of a pound of sugar to each pint of water; boil it until it is rich and thick; then add to it as many pints of the expressed juice of ripe blackberries as there are pounds of sugar; put half a nutmeg grated to each quart of the syrup; let it boil fifteen or twenty minutes, then add to it half a gill of fourth-proof brandy for each quart of syrup; set it by to become cold; then bottle it for use. A tablespoonful for a child, or a wineglass for an adult is a dose.

> * During the Civil War, Gail Borden produced a
> "condensed blackberry juice" using the same process
> with which he condensed milk. This condensed
> blackberry juice was used in Union hospitals for
> sick and wounded soldiers.

CARBONATED SYRUP WATER
[1860 AND 1862]

Put into a tumbler lemon, raspberry, strawberry, pineapple or any other acid syrup, sufficient in quantity to flavor the beverage very highly. Then pour in *very cold ice-water* till the glass is half full. Add half a teaspoonful of bicarbonate of soda (to be obtained at the druggist's), and stir it well in with a teaspoon. It will foam up immediately, and must be drank during the effervescence.

By keeping the syrup and the carbonate of soda in the house, and mixing them as above with ice-water, you can at any time have a glass of this very pleasant drink; precisely similar to that which you get at the shops.* The cost will be infinitely less.

> * Flavored soda waters (as well as soda
> counters where they were served) were
> firmly in place by the time the
> Civil War began.

COFFEE SYRUP
[1862]

This confection is exceedingly handy to travellers when proceeding on a long journey. Take half a pound of the best, roasted, ground coffee; boil the same in saucepan containing three quarts of water until the quantity is reduced to one quart; strain the latter off, and, when fined of all impurities, introduce the liquor into another clean saucepan, and let it boil over again, adding as much Lisbon sugar* to it as will constitute a thick syrup, like treacle; remove from the fire, and, when cold, pour it into bottles, corking the same tight down for use. Two teaspoonfuls of the syrup introduced into a moderate-sized teacup, and filled up with boiling water, will be fit for immediate use. If milk is at hand, use it *ad libitum*.

* Use regular granulated sugar.

NORWEGIAN RASPBERRY VINEGAR*
[1865]

[Shrub]

Take four pounds of raspberries, pour over them half a pint of vinegar, place it in an earthen jar, and cover it securely, so that no air can enter, and place it in a sunny window twelve hours; take it in at night, and place it out again in the sun the next day for another twelve hours.

Then place in a flannel bag, till the juice has run through without pressure. Then for every pound of juice take a pound of loaf sugar, and boil it for a quarter of an hour, or till no scum arises; then put it into small bottles, and well cork it.

> * This drink was made well into the twentieth century on New England farms, where it was used as a thirst-quencher. (I remember my mother taking a pitcherful to the hayfield where my father and the hired hands gratefully drank it down on hot, humid days in Vermont during the 1920s. —LMS)

Economy of the Tea Table
[1863]

As a test in general to distinguish genuine tea from the sloe-leaf, let it be infused, and some of the largest leaves spread out to dry; when the real tea-leaf will be found narrow in proportion to its length, and deeply notched at the edges with a sharp point, whilst the sloe-leaf is notched very slightly, is darker in color, rounder at the point, and of a coarser texture.

Presuming all ladies to be intimately acquainted with the mode of making tea, yet to some a few hints may be serviceable: —

First, never make tea in any other than a highly-polished teapot; for it is a chemical fact that metal retains the heat longer than earthenware, and the better it is polished the more completely will the liquid be kept hot, and the essence of the tea be extracted.

Secondly, see that the water be really boiling, not simmering, as is too commonly the case when taken from an urn, but kept either on the fire until boiled, or in one of those metal tea-kettles warmed by a spirit-lamp.

Tea retains its fine flavor better if kept in little tin canisters, instead of a caddy. It is impossible to prevent the admission of air into caddies; therefore it is better only to put a small quantity of tea into them at a time.

WATER-MELON SHERBET
[1863]

[A Bengal Recipe]

Let the melon be cut in half, and the inside of the fruit be worked up and mashed with a spoon, till it

assumes the consistency of a thick pulp. Introduce into this as much pounded white candy or sugar as may suit your taste, a wineglassful of fresh rose-water, and two wineglasses of sherry. Pour when strained, the contents into a jug and fill your tumblers as often as needed. This makes a very agreeable drink in summer.

BLACKBERRY WINE
[1860, 1861, AND 1862]

The following is said to be an excellent receipt for the manufacture of superior wine from blackberries: Measure your berries and bruise them, to every gallon adding one quart of boiling water; let the mixture stand for twenty-four hours, stirring occasionally; then strain off the liquor into a cask, to every gallon adding two pounds of sugar; cork tight, and let stand till following October*, and you will have wine ready for use, without any further straining or boiling, that will make lips smack as they never smacked, under similar influence, before.

* Blackberries are usually ripe in late July and August,
so the wine should stand for about three months.

BLACKBERRY AND WINE CORDIAL
[1860 AND 1862]

To half a bushel of blackberries, well mashed add a quarter of a pound of allspice, two ounces of cinnamon, two ounces of cloves; pulverize well, mix, and boil slowly until properly done; then strain or squeeze the juice through homespun or flannel, and add to each pint of the juice one pound of loaf-sugar; boil again for some time, take it off, and, while cooling add half a gallon of best Cognac brandy. Bottle and cork well. Dose: For an adult, half a gill to a gill; for a child, a teaspoonful or more, according to age.

This is recommended as a delightful beverage, and an infallible specific for diarrhoea or ordinary disease of the bowels.

GRAPE WINE
[1861]

To one gallon of grapes put one gallon of water; bruise the grapes, let them stand a week without stirring, then draw off, and fine.* Put to a gallon of wine three pounds of sugar, put it in a vessel; but it must not be stopped† till it has done hissing.

* Add three beaten egg whites.
† To "stop" means to bottle and cork.

RASPBERRY WINE
[1860, 1861, AND 1862]

Bruise the finest ripe raspberries with the back of a spoon; strain them through a flannel bag into a stone jar; allow one pound of fine powdered loaf-sugar to one quart of juice; stir these well together, and cover the jar closely; let it stand three days, stirring the mixture up every day; then pour off the clear liquid, and put two quarts of sherry to each quart of juice, or liquid. Bottle it off, and it will be fit for use in a fortnight. By adding Cognac brandy instead of sherry, the mixture will be raspberry brandy.

WHIPT SYLLABUBS*
[1861]

Stir gently one pint of scalded cream the same way until it becomes smooth and thick, but not to let it curdle, then add, while stirring, four ounces of loaf sugar rolled and sifted, the grated rind of one lemon, and the juice of two, two glasses of sherry wine, and, finally, the whites of three eggs beaten to a high froth with a small pine whisk. Fill your glasses, and, having left some syllabub in your bowl to raise the requisite froth for the tops of your filled glasses, begin and whisk it well, taking off every bubble, as it rises, with a teaspoon, placing it on the glass, and continuing to raise a pyramid of bubbles on each till enough to complete the light appearance. Syllabubs should be always made the day before they are to be eaten, and for a very pretty addition to the supper-table.

* At this time milk (and cream) were not pasteurized, thus the necessity for scalding the cream. Syllabub recipes exist back to the 1500s. "Bub" was a slang word for any bubbling drink. *The Yankee Cook Book* gives an 1808 recipe for a syllabub by Lucy Emerson of Montpelier, Vermont: "'Sweeten a quart of cyder with double refined sugar and grate nutmeg into it,' quoth Lucy. 'Then milk your cow into your liquor. When you have thus added what quantity of milk you think proper, pour half a pint or more, in proportion to the quantity of syllabub you make, of the sweetest cream you can get all over it'" (Wolcott 1939: 172).

CHEAP SMALL BEER
[1861]

To twelve quarts of cold water, add a pint and a half of strong hop tea, and a pint and a half of molasses. Mix it well together, and bottle it immediately. It will be fit for use the next day, if the weather is warm.

GINGER BEER QUICKLY MADE
[1861 AND 1862]

A gallon of boiling water is poured over three quarters of a pound of loaf-sugar, one ounce of ginger, and the peel of one lemon; when milk-warm, the juice of the lemon and a spoonful of yeast are added. It should be made in the evening, and bottled the next morning in stone bottles, and the cork tied down with twine.

Good brown sugar will answer, and the lemon may be omitted, if cheapness is required.

SPRUCE BEER
[1861]

Allow an ounce of hops and a spoonful of ginger to a gallon of water. When well boiled, strain it and put in a pint of molasses, and half an ounce or less of the essence of spruce; when cool add a teacup of yeast, and put into a clean tight cask and let it ferment for a day or two, then bottle for use. You can boil the sprigs of spruce-fir in room of the essence.

SOUPS

BACON AND CABBAGE SOUP
[1863]

Put your piece of bacon on to boil in a pot with two gallons (more or less, according to the number you have to provide for) of water, and when it has boiled up, and has been well skimmed, add the cabbages, kale, greens, or sprouts,* whichever may be used, well washed and split down,† and also some parsnips and carrots; season with pepper, but *no* salt, as the bacon will season the soup sufficiently: and when the whole has boiled together very gently for about two hours, take up the bacon surrounded with the cabbage, parsnips, and carrots, leaving a small portion of the vegetables in the soup, and pour this into a large bowl containing slices of bread; eat the soup first, and make it a rule that those who eat most soup are entitled to the largest share of bacon.

NOTE: Two quarts of soup is enough for 10 servings.

* Brussels sprouts

†Cut up in portions.

CHICKEN BROTH
[1868]

Cut up chicken; put it into an iron pot with two quarts of water, one onion, two tablespoonfuls of rice, a little salt, and boil it two hours; then strain it through a sieve. This will make one quart.

CHICKEN GUMBO*
[1861]

Cut up a young fowl as if for a fricassee. Put into a stew-pan a large tablespoonful of fresh butter, mixed with a teaspoonful of flour and an onion finely minced. Brown them over the fire, and then add a quart of water and the pieces of chicken, with a large quarter of a peck of ochras (first sliced thin and then chopped), and a salt-spoon† of salt. Cover the pan, and let the whole stew together till the ochras are entirely dissolved and the fowl thoroughly done. If it is a very young chicken, do not put it in at first, as half an hour will be sufficient to cook it. Serve it up hot in a deep dish.

You may add to the ochras an equal quantity of tomatoes cut small. If you use tomatoes, no water will be necessary, as their juice will supply a sufficient liquid.

* This southern dish had spread north by the time of the Civil War. "Gumbo" comes from the French word for okra. It was popularized by the French Acadians in Louisiana.

† Approximately 1/8 teaspoon.

CURRY SOUP
[1861]

Season two quarts of strong veal broth with two onions, a bunch of parsley, salt and pepper; strain it, and have ready a chicken, cut in joints and skinned; put it in the broth with a tablespoonful of curry powder; boil the chickens till quite tender. A little before serving add the juice of a lemon and a teacupful of boiling* cream. Always boil cream before putting it in the soup or gravy.

* Since we use pasteurized milk and cream, it would not be necessary to boil the cream.

CARROT SOUP
[1861]

Take six or eight full-grown carrots, of the red sort, scrape them clean, and rasp only the outer rind, or soft red part, and, if you have a single ripe tomato, add it, sliced, to the raspings, but use no other veg-etable except onions. While this is doing, the broth of any kind of fresh meat which has been got ready should be heated and seasoned with a couple of onions fried in butter, but without pepper, or any other seasoning, except a small quantity of mace and a little salt. When all is ready, put the raspings into two quarts of the skimmed broth, cover the stewpan close, and let it simmer by the side of the fire for two or three hours, by which time the raspings will have become soft enough to be pulped through a fine sieve; after which the soup should be boiled until it is as smooth as jelly, for any curdy appearance will spoil it.

Thus all the roots, and most of such vegetables as can be easily made into purees and combined with any sort of broth, will, in this manner, make excellent soup of different denominations, though all founded upon the same meat-stock. The gravy* of beef is always preferred for savory soups, and that of veal or fowls for the more delicate white soups; to which from half a pint to one pint of cream, or, if that cannot be had, the same quantity of milk and the yolks of two raw eggs, should be added for every two quarts of soup; remembering, however, that the latter will not impart the richness of cream.

* Stock. Today one can use canned chicken broth or consommé in place of stock.

A CHEAP GREEN PEA-SOUP
[1862]

Two quarts of green peas,* a piece of lean ham, some bones from roast meat; two onions sliced, two lettuces cut fine, a few sprigs of parsley, a bunch of sweet herbs;† put them to stew in two quarts of cold water, and let it simmer gentle. When quite tender, strain it, and pulp the peas and other vegetables through a sieve. Put it on the fire again, with pepper and salt, and about a pint of milk. Serve with fried bread cut into small dice.

* Probably these are dried, split peas.
† For sweet herbs use equal parts of parsley, tarragon, chives, and chervil, minced—about 1 tablespoon. Add

the herbs in the last few minutes of cooking, or they
can be tied in small cheesecloth bag and cooked with
the ham and peas, then removed. Fines herbes could
be substituted for the sweet herbs.

LETTUCE SOUP
[1863]

Cut up the white parts of two or four lettuces as needed, a quart of stock*, free from fat, and boiling; into this
throw the lettuces and a small onion, chopped very fine,
and a teaspoonful of salt; let it boil twenty minutes;
thicken with two tablespoonfuls of flour, first rubbed
smoothly in cold water, and a little soup added to it,
then strained before putting it to the soup, then throw
in a small bit of butter not larger than a walnut; let the
whole boil up once, and serve.

* Use chicken stock. Makes about 4 to 6 servings.

MOCK TURTLE SOUP
[1860]

Take a knuckle of veal, two cowheels, two large onions
stuck with cloves, one bunch of sweet herbs, spices, two
glasses of white wine, and a quart of water; put it into
an earthen jar, and stew for five hours; not to be opened
until cold; remove the fat and bones when all is carefully strained; if required for use, place it on the fire with
addition of forcemeat* balls and hard eggs; oysters, too,
may be added, and a very small quantity of anchovy

sauce. Cut the meat and fat an inch and a half square, and serve up in the soup.

* See the recipe on page 176.

MULLAGATAWNY SOUP*
[1862]

Cut up a knuckle of veal, and put it into a stewpan with a piece of butter, half a pound of lean ham, a carrot, a turnip, three onions, six apples; add half a pint of water. Set the stewpan on the fire, moving the meat round occasionally. Let it remain until the bottom of the stewpan is covered with a strong glaze; then add three table-spoonfuls of curry powder or curry paste, and half a pound of flour; stir well in, and fill the stewpan with a gallon of water. Add a spoonful† of salt and half a spoonful of sugar. When it boils, place it on the corner of the fire, and let it simmer two hours and a half, skimming off all fat as it rises.

*This soup, from a Tamil word meaning "pepper water," came to America from India by way of England. An earlier version appeared in Dr. Wm. Kitchiner's cookbook, *The Cook's Oracle,* in 1817.
†Teaspoonful.

MUSHROOM SOUP
[1870]

Take a good quantity of mushrooms, cut off the earthy end, and pick and wash them. Stew them with some butter, pepper, and salt in a little good stock* till tender;

take them out, and chop them up quite small; prepare a good stock as for any other soup, and add to it the mushrooms and the liquor they have been stewed in. Boil all together, and serve. If white soup be desired, use the white button mushrooms, and a good veal stock , adding a spoonful of cream or a little milk, as the color may require.

* Beef broth.
Chicken broth could be substituted.

Ochra Soup*
[1861]

Boil a leg of veal with about four dozen ochras, an hour, then add six tomatoes, six small onions, one green pepper, a bunch of thyme and parsley, and let it boil till dinner-time. Season it with salt and red pepper to your taste, and, if agreeable, add a piece of salt pork which has been previously boiled. The soup should boil seven or eight hours.

* This is an interesting recipe because it was one of the basic dishes served for "dinner" in places like Charleston, South Carolina, and yet today the recipe is difficult to find anywhere.

Potato Soup
[1860]

Have ready two quarts of boiling water. Cut up three or four potatoes, well pared, a thick slice or two of bread, six or eight leeks, well peeled and cut, as far as the white extends, into thin slices. Turn the whole into the water, which must be boiling at the time, cover, and let it come to a brisk boil after the ingredients are added, then throw in a teacupful (not a breakfast-cup*) of rice, a spoonful of salt, and half that of pepper. Boil slowly for an hour, or till all the ingredients amalga-mate.† Serve. This is a savory and cheap soup, very common in France and Germany. Cabbage soup is made in the same way, omitting the potatoes, and sub-stituting bread.

* A breakfast cup (approximately the size of
our coffee cup) was larger than a tea cup.
† Blend.

SHEEP'S HEAD SOUP
[1863]

Cut the liver and lights into pieces, and stew them in four quarts of water, with some onion, carrots, and turnips; half a pound of pearl barley, pepper and salt, cloves, a little marjoram, parsley, and thyme. Stew all these until nearly sufficiently cooked, then put in the head, and boil it until quite tender. Take it out, and strain everything from the liquor, and let it stand until cold, then remove the fat from the top. Before serving it must be thickened with flour and butter, as though it were mock turtle. A wineglassful of sherry should be put into the tureen before the soup is poured in. The heart cut into small pieces with rump steak makes an excellent pudding.

TOMATO SOUP
[1860]

Put in five quarts of water a chicken or a piece of any fresh meat, and six thin slices of bacon; let them boil for some time, skimming carefully, then throw in five or six dozen tomatoes peeled, and let the water boil away to about one quart, take out the tomatoes, mash and strain them through a sieve; mix a piece of butter, as large as a hen's egg, with a tablespoonful of flour, and add it to the tomatoes; season with salt and pepper; an onion or two is an improvement. Take the meat from the kettle when done, and put back the tomatoes. Let them boil half an hour. Lay slices of toasted bread in the tureen, and pour on the soup.

> * Since this would make an enormous amount, here is an alternate, smaller version: Cut in pieces a stewing chicken. Dip in flour. Sauté the bacon slices and brown the chicken pieces. Add only about two quarts of water and simmer until tender. Remove the chicken and chop the meat. Add one 1-lb., 12-oz. can of tomatoes, strained. Add one medium onion chopped fine, two tablespoons butter, and the chopped chicken meat. Add salt and pepper. Let simmer about 30 minutes. Makes about 10-12 cups.

WINTER SOUP
[1863]

Take carrots, turnips, and the heart of a head of celery, cut into dice, with a dozen button onions; half boil* them in salt and water, with a little sugar in it; then throw them into the broth; and, when tender, serve up the soup; or use rice, dried peas, and lentils, and pulp them into the soup to thicken it.

With many of these soups, small suet dumplings, very lightly made, and not larger than an egg, are boiled either in broth or water and put into the tureen just before serving, and are by most persons thought an improvement, but are more usually put in plain gravy-soup than any other, and should be made light enough to swim in it.

* Boil for approximately ten minutes.

OYSTER STEW
[1866]

To one hundred oysters, take one quart of milk, a half pint of water, four tablespoonfuls of flour, one tea-spoonful of salt, a half cup of butter and a little Cayenne pepper. Put the liquor of the oysters on to boil. Mix but-ter and flour and steam it in a bowl over the teakettle till soft enough to beat to a froth, then stir it into the liquor, after which add the other ingredients.

PEPPER-POT*
[1860 AND 1861]

Stew gently in four quarts of water till reduced to three, three pounds of beef, half a pound of lean ham, a bunch of dried thyme, two onions, two large potatoes pared and sliced; then strain it through a colander, and add a large fowl, cut into joints and skinned, half a pound of pickled pork,† sliced, the meat of one lobster, minced, and some small suet dumplings the size of a walnut. When the fowl is well boiled, add half a peck of spinach that has been boiled and rubbed through a colander; season with salt and Cayenne. It is very good without the lean ham and fowl.

> * This soup, often called Philadelphia Pepperpot, is said to have been created by a Pennsylvania Dutch cook in George Washington's army during the siege at Valley Forge (see Wason, 1962), but Karen Hess (in Randolph, 1984) believes it originated in the West Indies long before the Revolutionary War. It is noted for its use of tripe and cayenne pepper. This version does not use tripe, but rather salt pork.
> †Salt pork.

VERMICELLI, OR ITALIAN SOUP
[1863]

[*Minestrone*]

(*Made from stock from boiled bones.*) Take a quart of the stock, add a little salt, a little thickening made thus: take a teaspoonful of flour, roll it in a lump of butter the size of half a walnut, throw it into the cold stock; this will readily dissolve as it boils; then throw in an ounce of vermicelli, or Italian paste, which is cheaper, better, and prettier looking, being vermicelli cut into stars, cubes, and other similar shapes. When this has been boiled ten minutes, have ready a small tablespoonful of minced onion, throw this in, and let the soup boil five minutes; then pour some soup into a basin; burn a little brown sugar* in an iron spoon, mix it with the soup in the basin, then strain it to the soup. The onion may be omitted if desired. This soup will not take more than twenty minutes from the time it is first put on the fire.

* The brown sugar must be simply for color
and could be omitted.

CEREALS, BREADS, AND YEAST

HOMINY
[1864]*

There are three sizes of hominy. Large hominy requires to be boiled from four to five hours over a gentle fire. It should be washed clean, and put in the stewpan with just enough water to cover it. It is eaten as a vegetable. To cook the smaller hominy wash it in two waters; then to one teacupful of hominy add a quart of water and a teaspoonful of salt, and place the dish that contains it in a kettle of boiling water,† to prevent it from getting burnt, or else over a gentle fire. Let it boil for an hour, stirring it well with a spoon. It is generally eaten for breakfast. It is excellent, sliced and fried, after it has become cold.

* Hominy was a staple in the South
long before the Civil War.
† Use a double boiler.

TO MAKE HOMINY BREAD
[1860]

The hominy having been properly soaked, drain off the water, and add of fresh water seven and a half pints for each pound and a half of hominy, as weighed before soaking; let this simmer for four hours—if boiled rapidly, it will become hard and never swell; the hominy will then be fit for stir-about or bread. For bread, mix it gradually with the flour, making the dough in the ordinary way, and adding yeast in rather more than the usual proportion. This bread will keep moist and good for a longer time than if made entirely of wheaten flour.

PONE*
[1861]

Three eggs, a quart of Indian meal, a tablespoonful of fresh butter, a small teaspoonful salt, a half pint (or more) of milk. Beat the eggs until light and mix them with the milk. Then stir in gradually the Indian meal, adding the salt and butter. This must not be a batter, but a soft dough, just thick enough to be stirred well with a spoon. If too thin, add more Indian meal; if too stiff, thin it with a little more milk. Beat or stir it *long and hard*. Butter a tin or iron pan, put the mixture into it, and set the pan immediately into an oven, which must be moderately hot at first and the heat increased afterward. A Dutch oven is best for this purpose. It should bake an hour and a half or two hours, in proportion to its thickness. Send it to table hot and cut into slices. Eat it with butter and molasses.

* An Algonquian Indian word for a type of cornmeal bread, "pone" was primarily a southern dish.

To Dress Rice
[1860]

A lady recommends the following: Soak the rice in cold, salt water for seven hours; have ready a stewpan with boiling water, throw in the rice, and let it boil briskly for ten minutes; drain it in a colander, cover it up hot by the fire for a few minutes,* then serve. The grains will be found double the usual size, and quite distinct from each other.

99 LBS.NET WEIGHT
WHOLE BEAN
UNCOATED
TABLE RICE

* The rice can also be put in a hot oven at 350° for as long as 15 to 20 minutes.

Apple Fritters
[1862]

Peel and cut the apples into small pieces and stir them in with the batter. Fry all together as pancakes would be fried, about one fourth of an inch thick. Be careful to keep them from burning by having a sufficiency of lard in the pan, and by moving them frequently. Each fritter will take about five minutes to fry, and should look a pale brown when done.

CHEESIKINS
[1865]

Quarter pound stale bread, quarter pound cheese, two ounces butter, two eggs, a teaspoonful of mustard flour,* half teaspoonful of pepper, a few grains of Cayenne. Rub the bread into fine crums, grate the cheese, melt the butter, and mix with the rest of the ingredients, and the eggs, which should be previously beaten. Let the mixture stand for about an hour, and then knead it into a paste, roll it out very thin, cut into small pieces, and bake in a quick oven. Time, about fifteen or sixteen minutes.

* Ground mustard.

TO MAKE CREAM PANCAKES
[1863]

[Crepes]

Take the yelks of two eggs, mix them with half a pint of good cream and two ounces of sugar, heat the pan over a clear fire and rub it with lard, and fry the batter as thin as possible. Grate loaf sugar over them and serve them up hot.

COMMON CRULLERS OR TWIST CAKES*
[1863]

Mix well together half a pint of sour milk, or buttermilk, two teacupfuls of sugar, one teacupful of butter, and three eggs, well beaten; add to this a teaspoonful of saleratus dissolved in hot water, a teaspoon of salt, half a nutmeg grated, and a teaspoonful of powdered cinnamon; sift in flour enough to make a smooth dough: roll it out not quite a quarter of an inch thick, cut in small oblong pieces; divide one end in three or four parts like fingers, and twist or plait them over each other. Fry them in boiling lard. These cakes may be cut in strips, and the ends joined, to make a ring or in any other shape.

* Crullers were probably brought to the United States
by the Dutch who initially settled the Hudson Valley.

FRENCH PANCAKES
[1863]

[*Crepes*]

Beat half a pint of cream to a froth, lay it on a sieve; beat the whites and yelks (separately) of three eggs, add one tablespoonful of flour, and the same quantity of white sugar: Mix all lightly,* and bake in three saucers† for twenty minutes. Dish them up with raspberry or any other preserve, between.

* Fold in carefully.
† Or a small frying pan.

GERMAN SQUARES
[1862]

Rasp the crust well of a loaf, cut the crum into pieces about an inch thick and three inches square; soak these well in custard* for about two hours, turning them occasionally; then roll them in the rasped crust† and fry in a pan with lard. Serve with the following sauce in a separate boat. Beat the yolks and whites of two eggs on the fire, pouring in all the time very gently half a pint of white wine and sugar to taste. It should be served the moment it is finished, as being all in a froth it will spoil if it stands.

* I would use one beaten egg, ¼ cup milk,
2 tablespoons melted butter or salad oil, ⅛ teaspoon
salt. Soak it only long enough to coat the bread well.
—LMS.
† Bread crumbs.

INDIANA BATTER CAKES
[1865]

Sift into a pan three full pints of yellow* Indian corn meal; and add a large tablespoonful of fresh lard, or of nice roast-beef dripping well cleared from fat. Add a large teaspoonful of bicarbonate of soda, dissolved in a little warm water. Next make the whole into a soft  dough, with a pint of cold water. Afterwards thin it to the consistence of a moderate batter, by adding, gradually, not quite a pint and a half of warm water. When it is all mixed, continue to stir it well for about half an hour. Have ready a griddle heated over the fire, and bake the batter on it, in cakes, turning them when brown, send them to the table hot, and eat them with butter or molasses. These cakes are very light and good, and convenient to make, as they require neither eggs, milk, nor yeast. They may either be baked as soon as mixed, or they may stand for an hour or more.

* Northern cooks typically used yellow cornmeal, whereas southern cooks usually used white.

FOR MAKING SOUTH CAROLINA JOHNNY OR JOURNEY CAKE*
[1860]

Half a pint of boiled rice or hominy, two eggs, one tablespoonful of butter, a little salt, flour enough to make a stiff batter; spread on an oaken board, and bake before a hot fire; when nicely baked on one side, turn, and bake the other; cut through the centre, and butter well. It pays for the trouble. This is the way our servants made it at my home in Charleston, South Carolina.

* This may be an American version of the Scottish "bannock," the English "jannock" or "johnnick," which was made from oatmeal or wheat flour. Another possibility is that it was originally a food of slaves. According to the *Oxford English Dictionary,* the name first appeared in print in 1739.

ANOTHER JOHNNY CAKE RECEIPT*
[1860]

I see [sic] asked for a receipt for johnny cake. The one given [see above], made of rice or hominy, we call rice or hominy bread—that is, in the country, where johnny cake is made differently and a constant dish, also in this State (Florida). The true johnny cake is made of finely sifted meal salted and shortened with lard—or ham dripping, which gives a pleasant flavor—and made up, either with milk or warm water, to a consistency to prevent its falling from the board. Spread it equally, and place slanting before the fire till browned on both sides. Bread baked in this way has a very sweet taste.

> * This was probably the more common form of johnny cake. Note that both recipes call for cooking the bread on a wooden board slanted toward an open fire. The bread itself would have to be turned around on the board to cook evenly "on both sides."

SODA MUFFINS
[1862]

The following receipt affords a dish of light, spongy, most quickly-made muffins: To two pounds of flour add one teaspoonful of soda, ditto cream of tartar, and half a teaspoonful of sugar; mix thoroughly, with salt to taste, and make into a stiff batter with some milk; beat well for a few minutes. Have ready a hot earthenware pan, well buttered, also rings for the purpose. Pour in the batter, nearly half an inch thick; bake a nice brown on each side; either butter them and serve hot, or allow them to cool and toast before the fire.

Ramakins*
[1865]

Beat up well two eggs, and add two tablespoonfuls of flour, two ounces of warm butter, and two ounces of grated cheese. Mix all these well together, and bake them for a quarter of an hour in small boxes made of writing paper. They should be served hot in the paper boxes, and eaten after the game course. They require care in the preparation.

> * "Ramakins" comes from a word that meant toasted or baked cheese. It can also refer to the small individual dish (here the box) in which the cheese preparation is served.

Egg Dumplings
[1869]

Make a batter of a pint of milk, two well-beaten eggs, a teaspoonful of salt, and flour enough to make a batter as thick as for pound-cake. Have a clean saucepan of boiling water; let the water boil fast; drop in the batter with a tablespoon. Four or five minutes will boil them. Take them with a skimmer on a dish; put a bit of butter and pepper over them, and serve with boiled or cold meat. To serve sweet, put butter and grated nutmeg, with syrup or sugar over it.

POTATO DUMPLINGS
[1864]

The dumplings are made thus: Peel some potatoes and grate them into a basin of water; let the pulp remain in the water for a couple of hours, drain it off and mix with it half its weight of flour; season with pepper, salt, chopped onions and sweet herbs. If not moist enough, add a little water. Roll into dumplings the size of a large apple,* sprinkle them well with flour, and throw them into boiling water. When you observe them rising to the top of the saucepan, they will be boiled enough.

> * These would be easier to handle if they were smaller, and they would cook faster too.

YORKSHIRE PUDDING*
[1860 AND 1865]

Mix five spoonfuls of flour with a quart of milk and four eggs well beaten; butter a shallow pan, and bake under the meat; when quite brown, turn the other side upwards, and  brown that. It should be made in a square pan, and cut into pieces to come to table. It is a good plan to set over a chafing-dish at first, and stir it some minutes.

> * Although this dish is much older, a recipe for it appears in print in 1747: "Take a quart of Milk, four Eggs . . . make it up into a thick Batter with Flour, like a Pancake Batter" (*Oxford English Dictionary* 20:764). This pudding, of course, originated in Yorkshire, England, and was served before the main course. We now use it as a starch substitute in a meal.

BATH BUNS*
[1863]

Take a pound of flour, the rinds of three lemons, grated fine, half a pound of butter melted in a cup of cream, a teaspoonful of yeast, and three eggs. Mix; add half a pound of finely-powdered white sugar; mix well, let it stand to rise, and it will make thirty-nine buns.

* Bath buns originated in the fashionable spa of Bath on the southern coast of England. They are said to have been created by a Dr. Oliver who lived in Bath around 1750 (see FitzGibbon, 1976).

DOUGH NUTS
[1860, 1863, 1864, AND 1865]

Take a pound of flour, one-quarter pound of butter, three-quarters pound of brown sugar, one nutmeg grated, and a teaspoon of ground cinnamon; mix these well together; then add a tablespoon of bakers' yeast, and as much warm milk, with a bit of carbonate of potash about the size of a pea dissolved in it, as will make the whole into a smooth dough; knead it for a few minutes, cover it and set it in a warm place to rise, until it is light; then roll it out to one-quarter inch thickness, and cut it into small squares or diamonds, ready for cooking. Have ready a small iron kettle; put into it one pound of lard, and set it over a gentle fire. When it is boiling hot (*exactness* is required here), put the dough nuts in quickly, but one at a time; if the fat be of the right heat, the dough nuts will, in about ten minutes, be of a delicate brown outside, and nicely cooked inside. Keep the kettle in motion all the time the cakes are in, that they may boil evenly. When they are of a fine color, take them out with a skimmer, and lay them to drain on a sieve, turned upside down. If the fat be not hot enough, the cakes will absorb it; if too hot, they will be dark brown outside before the inside is cooked.

* Sometimes called "nutcakes," doughnuts were very popular in the North during this period, and Wiley (1952) reports that they were also favored by Union soldiers. They were served as an accompaniment to any meal—breakfast, dinner, or supper. Note that they were cut into squares or diamonds, not the "O" shape we use today.

GAUFFRES*
[1864]

[*Waffles*]

Take six new-laid eggs, one-half pound of fresh butter, one-half pint of cream, one-half pound of flour, a little yeast, and the rind of a lemon. Beat up the yolks of the six eggs with the butter, and add the cream, the flour, a teaspoonful of yeast, a little salt, a little rosewater, and the grated rind of one lemon. Mix all by beating up the batter thoroughly, and set it in a warm place, to rise, for an hour. Whisk up the whites of the six eggs and mix them with the batter, and bake the gauffres over a small stove till they are crisp.

* Both waffles and pancakes were of Dutch origin. "Gauffres" is the French word for waffles.

CRUMPETS*
[1861]

To a pint and a quarter
Of warm milk and water
Add one tablespoon of yeast
An egg and a small
Pinch of salt, and beat all
Up for twenty-two minutes at least;
Then set by the batter
To rise or grow fatter,
And, when it is ready, procure
A large ring† that will take
In a cupful, and bake
Till the top of it looks of a pure
Auburn color; then turn it,
Lest the oven should burn it;
And, as soon as the other side's brown
You may take it away
Without further delay,
And in like matter put others down.

* Recipes in *Godey's* occasionally appeared in verse.
†Muffin ring.

GRAHAM BREAD*
[1869]

Take one quart of warm water, one teacupful of good yeast, and one tablespoonful of salt; put into a pan; make a stiff batter with [Graham] flour which has been sifted,† and keep it very warm until light. Then take flour, which has been sifted, to thicken it; knead it well, but do not let it get cold; let it rise again. Then work it down, and put in one teacupful of sugar and a piece of butter the size of an egg; knead it half an hour; put in pans and let it rise very light. Bake three-quarters of an hour in a moderate oven.

* Graham bread is traceable to 1834 as any bread or biscuit made from unbolted wheat flour. It was named after the American dietary reformer Sylvester Graham. Whole wheat or *entire* wheat flour was formerly called graham flour. It contains all the parts of the wheat kernel, including the branny coats and the germ as well as the inner portion from which white flour is made.

† Graham flour need not be sifted today (see the following recipe).

GRAHAM BREAKFAST ROLLS
[1869]

To two pounds of peeled potatoes, boiled soft and mashed through a cullender, add one pint of water, half a cupful of sugar, one large teaspoonful of salt, and half a cupful of soft yeast (or the quantity required to raise the dough if in any other form). Mix with Graham flour into a rather stiff loaf, let it rise over night; mound into small cakes in the morning, and when light, bake. Never sift your Graham flour.

BROWN BREAD*
[1865]

One quart of corn meal, wet thoroughly with boiling-water; then add one quart of lukewarm water, one quart of raw corn-meal, one quart of Graham flour, one tablespoonful of salt, four tablespoonfuls good hop yeast, one teacupful of molasses; mix thoroughly; when light, bake two hours in a moderately heated oven.

* An old traditional New England favorite, this bread
is now usually steamed rather than baked.

HOT CROSS BUNS*
[1862 AND 1865]

Rub a quarter pound of butter into two pounds of flour, quarter of a pound of brown sugar, mix all well together; a pint of new milk made warm, three well-beaten eggs, one tablespoonful of yeast, one tablespoonful of soda, one pound of currants, one ounce of candied lemon, one ounce of citron, a little lemon-peel and salt; make all up into a light paste, set it by the fire to rise an hour, and make it into buns; twenty minutes will bake them.

* Buns of this type were served in England in pre-
Christian times to herald the goddess of spring, but
small hot cross buns date back to England of the
1300s and were served on Good Friday. They were
allegedly given to churchgoing travelers for Easter
Sunday and traditionally have a cross marked on top.

SALLY LUNNS*
[1862]

A pint of the best, new milk lukewarm, add to it one-quarter of a pound of butter, a little salt, a teacupful of yeast, one and a half pound of fine flour; mix them together, and let it stand three-quarters of an hour. Bake them on tins nearly an hour.

> * Sally Lunn was a young woman who cried her wares through the streets of Bath in England around 1790. Her wares included a variant of this cake, and they were so popular that her business was bought up by a baker and musician named Dalmer. He supposedly made up a song about her and her famous "bun." Sally Lunn is still a popular cake, especially in the South. The original Sally Lunn bun was baked in a pan with a tube center (the original Turk's head).

TEA BUNS
[1862]

One pound and a quarter of flour, one-half pound of currants (well washed), two ounces of butter rubbed in the flour, about a pint of sweet milk warmed, two

spoonsful of yeast, the yolk of an egg well beaten, car-raway seeds to your taste; mix well these ingredients together and beat them up as for a seed cake; set them before the fire to rise for an hour, make them up in what shaped cakes you please, lay them on tin plates for a time before the fire, and feather* them over with white of egg before baking them.

* Brush lightly with a pastry brush.

WATER CAKES*
[1862]

Two eggs beaten very lightly, one pint of cold water, one teaspoonful of salt, flour to make it as thick as fritters, bake half an hour in a hot oven; eat with butter; bake in little tins filled full.

* This is probably a wartime recipe.

FOR MAKING YEAST*
[1860]

Put three quarts of water into a boiler, and one pint of hops tied up in a thin material to let the strength boil out of them; let them boil an hour, adding to the water, as soon as it boils, one tablespoonful of ginger, two of salt, and two of molasses. After boiling the hops suffi-ciently, take them out; stir up a thickening of flour and water sufficient to make your yeast about as thick as paste; stir this into the water, and let it boil up once; take it out, and let it stand till lukewarm; then add your old yeast to make it rise. When fermented, put it away in a jug. This yeast will keep two months. When you wish to make bread, take half a teacupful of yeast, put in your mixing-pan, add one pint of warm water, and stir in the flour; set the sponge in a warm place to rise in cold weather; in the morning, add a little salt and half a pint of warm milk, and mix the bread; when risen again, mould it up, put in pans, and let it stand about one hour, when it is ready to bake. This receipt is all it is recommended to be.

* Most recipes today call for some sugar to be added,
which speeds up the yeast activity;
too much sugar suppresses it.

How to Make Yeast
[1860]

Boil one pound of good flour, quarter of a pound of brown sugar, and a little salt in two gallons of water, for one hour. When milk-warm, bottle it and cork it close. It will be ready for use in twenty-four hours. One pint of this yeast will make eighteen pounds of bread.

EGGS AND CHEESE

ANOTHER METHOD OF COOKING EGGS
[1864]

[or a Rechauffe]

This dish is particularly suitable to invalids and little children who are not of an age to masticate their food. All the nutritive qualities of the eggs are preserved, together with the lightness of the omelette.

The requisite number of eggs is beaten, seasoned, and passed through a sieve, to which a small quantity of good gravy* is added. The mixture must be placed in an enamelled stewpan, and set over a slow fire till the eggs thicken. The stewing pan is then removed and a small piece of fresh butter is added to the mixture, which, when melted, is ready to receive the addition of any finely minced fowl, meat, fish, asparagus, pease or cauliflower, that may be desired. The latter ingredients must be stirred in until warm through, but not suffered to boil.

* Gravy means broth.

Eggs au Buerre Noir
[1867]

Heat some butter in a frying pan until it is of a good dark-brown color; break six or eight eggs into a dish; season them to be of any particular flavor desired, and slide them gently into the frying-pan. When done, turn them carefully into a dish; pour a good tablespoonful of strong white-wine vinegar into the frying-pan, bring it quickly to a boil, pour it upon the eggs, and serve hot as possible.

Eggs aux Fines Herbes
[1867]

Boil some eggs for rather less than five minutes, then plunge them into cold water, and afterwards remove the shells; arrange the eggs in a dish, and pour over them a sauce made as follows: Mix two ounces of butter with a little flour, and put it into a stewpan with some finely-shread parsley and shallot; salt and pepper; warm it up quickly; moisten it with white wine, and let it simmer until it has acquired the proper consistency. The eggs and the sauce should be prepared simultaneously, so as to serve the dish hot.

A Good Way of Cooking Eggs
[1864]

Boil say six eggs quite hard, peel, and cut in two lengthways; put two ounces of good butter in a saucepan (enameled the best), boil till of a rich brown; have ready to hand a tablespoonful of vinegar mixed with a teaspoonful of made mustard, salt and pepper to taste, and pour this mixture into the boiling butter, mix well and pour over the eggs (which must be kept hot) so that each portion of egg receives its share of sauce; the eggs should be placed on the dish with the yelk part upwards, and serve up immediately, as hot as possible; the sauce must be well blended, and for this purpose use a small pastebrush; a teaspoonful of water will often facilitate the blending. The same sauce is excellent with boiled fish. 6 Servings.

How to Eat an Egg
[1860]

There is an old saying, taken from the Italian, "Teach your grandmother to suck eggs." This appears an unnecessary piece of information, as people do not suck eggs as they do oranges; but as we believe there are few who know how to eat one properly, we shall give the secret. By the usual mode of introducing the salt it will not mix or incorporate with the egg, the result is, you either get a quantity of salt without egg, or egg without salt. Put in a drop or two of water, tea, coffee, or other liquid you may have on the table at the time, then add the salt, and stir. The result is far more agreeable; the drop of liquid is not tasted.

EGGS FRITS
[1862]

[*Fried Eggs*]

Break some eggs into a frying-pan of hot friture,* and, before the yelks become hard, take them up, and serve them upon a good gravy, or on a toast sprinkled with ketchup, or with a sauce of any kind.

> * "Friture" is a French word used either for the fat,
> oil, butter, or drippings in which fish, meat,
> or anything else is to be fried, or for the fried food
> out of the frying pan. "Friture" is also used for
> the fat in deep frying.

POACHED EGGS
[1863]

Poached eggs make several excellent dishes, but poaching them is rather a delicate operation, as in breaking the egg into the water particular care must be taken to keep the white round the yelk. The best way is to open the small end of the egg with a knife. When the egg is done (it must be very soft), it should be thrown into cold water, where it may be pared, and its appearance improved before it is dished up. Poached eggs are served up upon spinach, or stewed endive, or alone with rich gravy, or with stewed Spanish onions. They may also be fried in oil until they are brown, when they form a good dish with rich gravy.

A German Entremet
[1865]

Boil eight eggs quite hard, and when cold cut them in two lengthwise. Take the yelks out very carefully, pass them through a fine sieve, and mix them well with half a pint of cream (or more if required), and then add pepper, salt, and herbs. Pour this sauce into a very flat pie-dish that will stand heat, and place the white half eggs carefully in it, arranging them in the form of a star, or any other pattern preferred. Fill up the vacancy left in them by the yelks having been removed, with the same mixture, and strew a few breadcrums over them. Bake this very slightly, just enough to give it a bright yellow color, and serve it up in the dish in which it has been baked.

Rumbled* Eggs
[1866]

Very convenient for invalids, or when required, a light dish for supper. Beat up three eggs with two ounces of fresh butter, or well-washed salt butter; add a teaspoonful of cream or new milk. Put all in a saucepan and keep stirring it over the fire for nearly five minutes, until it rises up like a souffle, when it should be immediately dished on buttered toast.

> * Probably from "rumple," meaning
> wrinkled or crumpled.

EGGS AND SAUSAGE
[1867]

Cut some slices of Bologna or Spanish sausage; toss them in butter or olive oil. Fry some eggs, trim them nicely, and lay one upon each piece of sausage; arrange among them some parsley leaves, fried crisp, and serve as hot as possible.

A SPRING DISH
[1860]

[*Spinach*]

Upon a toasted bread place a layer of well-boiled spinach about an inch thick; upon this place at equal distances poached eggs. This forms a pretty, light, and nourishing dish; but be careful that the yellow of the egg is not broken, or the appearance will be lost, and the eggs not worth eating.

EGGS STEWED WITH CHEESE
[1864]

Fry three eggs in a pan with one ounce of butter, seasoned with pepper and salt, and when the eggs are just set firm at the bottom of the pan, slip them off on to a dish, cover them all over with some very thin slices of cheese, set the dish before the fire to melt the cheese, and then eat this cheap little tit-bit with some toast.

A BENGAL OMELET
[1862]

Take half a dozen fresh eggs, beat the whites and yolks up well together in a clean basin; chop half a dozen young onions fine, a little fresh parsley, three green chilies,* and add a teaspoonful of catsup. Mix all together, and fry them after the form of a pancake. When done, brown, take a fork to roll them up, and send to table.

* This recipe is unique for its use of chilies.

BUTTERED EGGS
[1865]

Take three eggs, beat them up well, then add to them a gill of sweet milk. Place some butter (about the size of a large walnut) at the bottom of a pan, pour the mixture into it, and boil until quite thick. Pour it upon buttered toast, and grate some ham or beef over it.

BREAD OMELETTE
[1864]

Break six eggs, season them with pepper and salt, or sweeten with sugar, if preferred; add a good table-spoonful of finely grated bread crums made of stale bread. Beat the whole well together, and fry in the same manner as the plain omelette. This omelette requires a little more attention in the dressing than those which are made out of bread, being more liable to burn and break. It is an excellent accompaniment to preserve apricot, or any other description of rich jam.

OMELETTE SOUFFLÉE
[1864]

Break six eggs, and separate the whites from the yelks. Add to the latter some sifted sugar, flavored with lemon-peel. Beat the yelks and sugar, then whisk the whites. Pour the yelks and whites together, continuing the whisking until the eggs froth. Melt a little butter in the omelette pan, and place it over a slow fire. When the butter is melted (but not hot), pour in the mixture, and gently shake the pan until the top of the mixture falls to the bottom. When the butter is dried up, fold the omelette on a buttered dish, sift a little sugar on the top, and brown with a salamander.

The above soufflée may be varied in endless ways by adding different flavorings, or preserved fruit, at the time of beating the yelks of the eggs.

CHEESE CREAM
[1862]

[A Plain Family Way]

Put three pints of milk to one half pint of cream, warm or according to the same proportions, and put in a little rennet;* keep it covered in a warm place till it is curdled; have a mould with holes, either of china or any other; put the curds into it to drain about an hour; serve with a good plain cream and pounded sugar over it.

* Use a rennet tablet.

POTTED CHEESE (RICH)
[1860]

Pound well six ounces of rich cheese, *not decayed;* add one ounce and a half of fresh butter, a teaspoonful of white powdered sugar, some pounded mace, to taste, and a large wineglassful of any strong white wine. Mix all together, then press down in small, deep pots, or one deep pot, taking out for use a little at a time. It will keep good a long time.

MACCARONI CHEESE
[1861]

[*simply done*]

Boil the maccaroni in milk; put in the stewpan butter, cheese, and seasoning; when melted, pour into the maccaroni, putting breadcrums over, which brown before the fire all together.

WELSH RABBIT*
[1863]

A slice of bread laid in a tin dish, buttered, and mustard laid over it; pieces of cut cheese laid also on the bread and butter: pour two or three tablespoonfuls of ale; put into the oven until slightly brown.

* Originally a humorous name at the expense of the Welsh, this dish is now often called "rarebit."

VEGETABLES

VEGETABLES
[1865 AND 1868]

Vegetables should be carefully cleaned from insects and nicely washed. Boil them in plenty of water, and drain them the moment they are done enough. If overboiled they will lose their beauty and crispness. Bad cooks sometimes dress them with meat, which is wrong, except carrots or cabbage with boiling beef.

In order to boil vegetables of a good green color, take care that the water boils when they are put in. Make them boil very fast. Do not cover, but watch them, and if the water has not slackened you may be sure they are done when they begin to sink. Then take them out immediately, or the color will change. Hard water, especially if chalybeate, spoils the color of such vegetables as should be green. To boil them green in hard water, put a teaspoonful of carbonate of soda* or potash into the water when it boils, before the vegetables are put in.

Potatoes are good with all meats. With fowls they are nicest mashed. Carrots, parsnips, turnips, greens, and cabbage are eaten with boiled meat; and beets, peas, and beans are appropriate to either boiled or roasted meat. Mashed turnip is good with roasted pork. Tomatoes are good with every kind of meat, but especially so with roast.

* Cooks today do not add soda when cooking vegetables; it destroys much of the vitamin and mineral content.

FRIED ARTICHOKES
[1867]

Cut the artichokes into six or eight pieces, according to their size, remove the choke and the large leaves which will not become tender, and trim off the tops of the remainder of the leaves with a pair of scissors. Wash them in several waters, drain them, and dip them in a batter made with flour, a little cream, and the yelk of an egg. Let the artichokes be well covered with the batter, and fry them in lard. Sprinkle a little salt over them, and serve them on a bed of parsley fried in the lard which remains in the pan.

BEANS IN A FRENCH STYLE
[1869]

Choose small young beans, and strip off the ends and stalks, throwing them, as prepared, into a dish full of cold spring water, and, when all are finished, wash and drain them well. Boil them in salted boiling water, in a large saucepan, and drain them, after which put them into an enamelled stewpan, and shake them over the fire until they are quite hot and dry; then add about three ounces of fresh butter, and a tablespoonful of veal or chicken broth; the butter must be broken up into small lumps. Season with white pepper, salt, and the juice of half lemon strained. Stir them well over a hot fire for five minutes, and serve them in a vegetable dish very hot.

BUTTERED CABBAGE
[1862]

Boil the cabbage with a quantity of onions, then chop them together, season with pepper and salt, and fry them in butter. It is a rather homely, but savory dish, and frequently used either with fried sausages laid over it or as an accompaniment to roast beef, and forms part of bubble and squeak.

To Stew Carrots
[1860]

Half boil the carrots, then scrape them nicely, and cut them into thick slices; put them into a stewpan, with as much milk as will barely cover them, a very little salt and pepper, and a sprig or two of chopped parsley; simmer them till they are perfectly tender, but not broken; when nearly done, add a piece of fresh butter rolled in flour. Send them to the table hot. Carrots require long cooking. Parsnips and salisfy may be stewed in the above manner, substituting a little chopped celery for the parsley.

Dressing for Cabbage
[1864]

[Hot Slaw]

Cut your cabbage fine in a dish* and sprinkle salt and pepper over it, take one egg, a teaspoonful of sugar, one-half spoonful of flour, one-half teacup of sweet cream, the same of vinegar, a very small piece of butter. Beat all together, and let it boil; then pour over the cabbage while hot.

* Soak in cold water for one hour.

Cauliflower Omelet
[1860]

Take the white part of a boiled cauliflower after it is cold, chop it very small, and mix with it a sufficiency

[*sic*] quantity of well-beaten egg to make a very thick batter; then fry it in fresh butter in a small pan, and send it hot to table.

CELERY SAUCE, WHITE
[1863]

[Celery cooked with sauce added]
Pick and wash two heads of nice white celery; cut it into pieces about an inch long; stew it in a pint of water, and a teaspoonful of salt, till the celery is tender; roll an ounce of butter with a tablespoonful of flour; add this to half a pint of cream, and give it a boil up.

TO STEW CELERY
[1862]

Take off the outside, and remove the green ends from the celery; stew in milk and water until they are very tender. Put in a slice of lemon, a little beaten* mace and thicken with a good lump of butter and flour; boil it a little, and then add the yelks of two well-beaten eggs mixed with a teacupful of good cream. Shake the saucepan over the fire until the gravy thickens, but do not let it boil. Serve it hot.

* Grated or ground.

To Dress Cucumbers
[1861]

Pare one or two cucumbers, cut it equally into very thin slices, and commence cutting from the thick end; if commenced at the stalk, the cucumber will most likely have an exceedingly bitter taste, far from agreeable. Put  the slices into a dish, sprinkle over salt and pepper, and pour over 3 tablespoonfuls of salad oil, and 4 of vinegar, in these proportions; turn the cucumber about, and it is ready to serve. This is a favourite accompaniment to boiled salmon, and makes a pretty garnish to lobster salad.

Corn Oysters*
[1860]

Grate four ears of green corn; beat the whites of five eggs separate, and beat the yolks also separate; stir in the yellow of the eggs with the grated corn; add two cups of flour, and milk enough to make a batter for griddle cakes. Add one-half teaspoonful of soda; when all is well mixed, add the whites of the eggs. Bake on griddles.

* This recipe may have been developed by
Shaker cooks. A version of it can still be
found in cookbooks today.

GREEN CORN DUMPLINGS
[1867]

A quart of young corn grated from the cob, half a pint of wheat flour sifted, half a pint of milk, six tablespoonfuls of butter, two eggs, a saltspoonful of salt, a saltspoonful of pepper, and butter for frying. Having grated as fine as possible sufficient young fresh corn to make a quart, mix with it the wheat flour, and add the salt and pepper. Warm the milk in a small saucepan, and soften the butter in it. Then add them gradually to the pan of corn, stirring very hard, and set it away to cool. Beat the eggs light, and stir them into the mixture when it has cooled. Flour your hands and make it into little dumplings. Put into a frying-pan a sufficiency of fresh butter (or lard and butter in equal proportions), and when it is boiling hot, and has been skimmed, put in the dumplings, and fry them ten minutes or more, in proportion to their thickness. Then drain them, and send them hot to the dinner table.

USES OF THE DANDELION
[1862]

Its uses are endless: the young leaves blanched make an agreeable and wholesome early salad; and they may be boiled, like cabbages, with salt meat. The French too slice the roots and eat them, as well as the leaves with bread and butter, and tradition says that the inhabitants of Minorca once subsisted for weeks on this plant, when their harvest had been entirely destroyed by insects. The leaves are ever a favorite and useful article of food in the Vale of Kashmir, where, in spite of the preconceived prejudices we all have to the contrary, dandelions, and other humbler examples of our northern "weeds," do venture to associate themselves with the rose or the jasmine of its eastern soil. On the banks of the Rhine the plant is cultivated as a substitute for coffee, and Dr. Harrison contends that it possesses the fine flavor and substance of the best Mocha coffee, without its injurious principle; and that it promotes sleep when taken at night, instead of banishing it, as coffee does. Mrs. Modie gives us her experiences with dandelion roots, which seem of a most satisfactory nature. She first cut the roots into small pieces, and dried them in the oven until they were brown and crisp as coffee, and in this state they appear to have been eaten. But certain it is that she ground a portion of them, and made a most superior coffee.* In some parts of Canada they make an excellent beer of the leaves, in which the saccharine matter they afford forms a substitute for malt, and the bitter flavor serves instead of hops. In medicine, too, it is invaluable.

* In Europe dandelion roots (dried, roasted, and ground) are often still added to ground coffee.

EGGPLANT
[1867]

Select long purple if possible, the next kind is the round kind with prickles on the stem. Peel and slice them, spread salt on each separate piece and lay them in a colander to drain; let them lie one hour, parboil, and fry them, until thoroughly cooked, in pork fat or butter; eggplant, unless well cooked, are insipid and even disgusting; they must be cooked through and browned.

FRENCH STEW OF PEAS AND BACON
[1867]

Cut about one-quarter of a pound of fresh bacon into thin slices; soak it on the fire in a stewpan until it is almost done; then put about a quart of peas to it, a good bit of butter, a bunch of parsley, and two spoonfuls of catsup,* simmer on a slow fire and reduce the sauce; take out the parsley and serve the rest together.

* A teaspoon or two of Worcestershire sauce may be used in place of catsup.

Lettuce Peas
[1865]

Having washed four lettuces, and stripped off the outside leaves, take their hearts, and (having chopped them
well) put them into a stewpan with two quarts of young
green peas, freshly shelled; a lump or two of loaf-sugar;
and three or four leaves of green mint minced as finely
as possible. Then put in a slice of cold ham, and a quarter of a pound of butter divided into four bits and rolled
in flour; and two tablespoonfuls of water. Add a little
black pepper, and let the whole stew for about twenty-
five minutes, or till the peas are thoroughly done. Then
take out the ham, and add to the stew half a pint of
cream. Let it continue stewing five minutes longer. Then
send it to table.

Onion Custard
[1860 and 1861]

Peel and slice some mild onions (ten or twelve, in proportion to their size), and fry them in fresh butter,
draining them well when you take them up; then
mince them as fine as possible; beat four
eggs very light, and stir them gradually
into a pint of milk, in turn with the
minced onions; season the whole
with plenty of grated nutmeg, and stir
it very hard; then put it into a deep
white dish, and bake it about a quarter of

an hour.* Send it to table as a side dish, to be eaten with meat or poultry. It is a French preparation of onions, and will be found very fine.

* Bake at 350° 50 to 60 minutes.

ONION SAUCE
[1862]

[Boiled Onions]

Boil the onions until tender, changing the water occasionally to render them more mild. Strain, and mash the onions in a bowl; adding butter and salt. Warm up again and mix the whole thoroughly.

YOUNG ONION SAUCE
[1863]

[Boiled Young Onions]

Peel a pint of button onions, and put them in water till you want to put them on to boil; put them into a stewpan, with a quart of cold water; let them boil till tender; they will take (according to their size and age) from half an hour to an hour.

TO FRY PARSLEY
[1861]

When the parsley has been washed and thoroughly dried, throw it into lard or butter which is on the point to boil; take it up with a slice the instant it is crisp, and lay it on paper on a sieve before the fire.

To Crisp Parsley
[1861]

Pick some bunches of young parsley, wash them, and swing them in a cloth to dry; put them on a sheet of paper in a toaster before the fire, and keep them frequently turned till they are quite crisp, which will be in about six or eight minutes.

Parsnep Fritters
[1862]

Boil six parsneps tender; then skin and mash them, mix with them one or two eggs well beaten, and two teaspoonfuls of wheat flour. Make them up in small cakes, and fry them in a little lard or beef gravy, made boiling hot before the cakes are put in. A little salt should be added to the lard or gravy.

About Potatoes
[1863]

Many good cooks are bad managers of potatoes, and this esculent, which in most houses is served every day, and which is so popular in many families as to be often the only vegetable at table, requires much care in the cooking. The great fault in cooking potatoes, whether they are steamed or boiled, is allowing them, when they are cooked, to sodden in the moisture still hanging about the vessel in which they have been cooked, or in the steam which they give out. If they are boiled, as soon as they are cooked enough they should be taken out of the saucepan (an iron pot is best for the purpose), which should be emptied and *wiped out dry:* the potatoes being then returned to it will dry and become mealy. If they are steamed, take the steamer off the kettle as soon as the potatoes are cooked enough and place it on a hot plate, in a side oven, or anywhere else where they will keep very hot, and where they will dry. The grand items with potatoes are, develop their mealiness by allowing the moisture to evaporate, serve them very hot, and serve but a few at a time, so that relays of hot dishes of them may be ready to go in with every fresh course with which they are at all likely to be required.

POTATO BALLS
[1863]

Take four potatoes, boiled the day before, grate (not rub) them. Add two tablespoonfuls of flour and two eggs, salt, and a *very* little nutmeg. Make into round balls, put them into boiling water, and boil twenty minutes.* Oil some butter and brown some chopped onions in it. When balls are finished, throw them over raspings of bread, and then pour on the hot oil and onions. N. B. The great point is to serve very hot.

* Since the potatoes are already cooked, it would not be necessary to boil for twenty minutes.

POTATO CHIPS*
[1865]

Wash and peel some potatoes, then pare them, ribbon-like, into long lengths; put them into cold water to remove the strong potato flavor; drain them, and throw them into a pan with a little butter, and fry them a light brown. Take them out of the pan, and place them close to the fire on a sieve lined with clean writing paper to dry, before they are served up. A little salt may be sprinkled over them.

* This recipe marks one of the earliest appearances in print of potato chips.

POTATOES MASHED WITH ONIONS
[1862]

Prepare some boiled onions by putting them through a sieve, and mix them with potatoes. In proportioning the onions to the potatoes, you will be guided by your wish to have more or less of their flavor.

NEW POTATOES A LA FRANCAISE
[1867]

Skin, wash and wipe dry some early potatoes; melt some butter in a stew pan; when it is quite hot place the potatoes in it, simmer them slowly, turn them occasionally, and when done take them up and place them in another stew pan, with sufficient fresh butter to form a sauce, shake them over the fire merely till the butter is melted, arrange them in a dish, pour the butter over them and stew a little fine salt upon them, serve as hot as possible. In Italy olive oil is employed instead of butter, and is really preferable.

POTATO SALAD [HOT]
[1861 AND 1865]

Boil as many potatoes as will make a dish for your family; when done, peel them carefully, and slice while hot into a deep dish; cut in very small pieces young onions or shives,* and mix them among the slices, distributing a little pepper and salt; pour over the whole, good vinegar, scalding hot, and send it to the table immediately. A wholesome and pleasant dish for spring and early summer.

* Chives.

SPINACH
[1864]

When carefully washed and picked, place in a saucepan just large enough to hold it, sprinkle it with a little salt, and cover close. Shake well while on the fire. When done, beat up the spinach with a piece of butter. A spoonful of cream improves the flavor.

Sweet Potatoes* a l'Allemande
[1867]

Boil or steam some potatoes very nicely, peel them, cut them in slices, cut some bread into similarly-sized pieces (without any crust), butter a tart dish, line it with bread and potatoes, alternating them regularly. Thicken some scalding hot milk with a sufficiency of potato flour, add sugar and bruised bay or laurel leaves to impart a flavor, put it into the dish and strew some sugar upon the top. Place it in an oven until slightly browned on the surface.

* Use white potatoes. These are called "sweet" because of the use of sugar.

Succotash*
[1860]

Take of Indian corn, not ground, one pint, and the same quantity of white (haricot) beans. Rinse the corn in cold water and put it into a basin with water enough to cover it; put the beans also to soak in a basin, with water to cover them; let them remain until the next day. Within two hours of dinner time pour the water from the beans, pick out any bad ones, and put them with the corn, and the water in which it was soaked, into the boiler. Cut a nicely-salted pork into thin slices; put it to the corn and beans, and put over them hot water, rather more than to cover them; add a little Cayenne and cover the pot close: set it where it will boil very gently for an hour and a half, then put it into a deep dish; add a bit of butter to it, and serve up. The pork may be put in whole, if preferred, and served as a separate dish; or the corn and beans may be cooked without the pork. In the latter case, season with salt and pepper, and add plenty of butter.

> * According to Imogene Wolcott in *The Yankee Cook Book,* the word "M'sickquatash" (the Narragansett Indian word for corn boiled whole) became the "succotash" of the Pilgrims when they combined corn and beans. As time went on, however, succotash developed into a more elaborate dish made of large white beans, hulled corn, corned beef, salt pork, chicken, white turnip, and potatoes, and in this form was a famous food of Plymouth, Massachusetts, where it was served again and again at celebrations of Forefathers' Day, December 21.

BROWNED TOMATOES*
[1865]

Take large round tomatoes and halve them; place them, the skin side down, in a frying-pan in which a very small quantity of butter or lard has been previously melted; sprinkle them with salt and pepper and dredge them well with flour, and let them brown thoroughly; then stir them and let them brown again, and so on until they are quite done. They lose their acidity, and the flavor is superior to stewed tomatoes.

> * Tomatoes originated in tropical America and were probably used first in the South. Karen Hess in her notes to *The Virginia House-Wife* suggests that they were not considered poisonous in the nineteenth century despite stories to the contrary. Indeed, *Godey's* gives several tomato recipes.

TURNIPS
[1862]

Should always be boiled whole, and put in much after either carrots or parsnips, as they require less boiling. When used in stews, they are cut into small pieces the size of dice, or made into shapes with a little instrument to be found at all cutlery shops.

They may be mashed in the same manner as parsnips; but some persons add the yelk of a raw egg or two. They are also frequently made into a puree to thicken mutton broth.

TURNIPS IN GRAVY
[1862]

To a pound of turnips sliced and cut into dice, pour a quarter pint of boiling veal gravy, add a small lump of sugar, some salt and cayenne, or white pepper, and boil them quickly 50 to 60 minutes. Serve them very hot.

VEGETABLE CURRY
[1862]

Take carrots, turnips, celery, onions, some cucumbers and lettuce, cut small and simmer for a considerable time in water. Have ready some good gravy properly seasoned, and add the vegetables to it. When sufficiently stewed, mix in a piece of butter with flour to give it a proper thickness, a tablespoonful of curry-powder, and the juice of a small lemon. Give it a boil, and when serving up add a dessertspoonful of mushroom catsup.*

> * Mushroom catsup: Chop mushrooms. Sprinkle salt over each layer. Simmer, stirring often. Strain juice off and boil it with a little ginger. Add pepper. Use juice without adding water.

VEGETABLE OYSTER CAKES
[1862]

[*Salsify*]
Select good, large-sized oyster plant roots, grate them, and add milk and flour sufficient to make a stiff batter,

about a gill of grated oyster plant, two eggs, one pint of milk, and flour to make the batter, and salt. Drop it by tablespoonfuls into hot lard. Bake till brown.

WINTER SQUASH
[1862]

This requires rather more boiling than the summer kind. Pare it, cut it in pieces, take out the seeds and strings; boil it in a very little water till it is quite soft. Then press out the water, mash it, and add butter, salt, and pepper to your taste. From half to three-quarters of an hour will generally suffice to cook it.

SALAD DRESSINGS
AND SAUCES

BREAD SAUCE
[1862]

Boil the crum of bread with a minced onion and some whole white pepper [corns]; when the onion is cooked, take it out, as also the peppercorns, and put the bread, carefully crushed through a sieve, into a saucepan with cream, a little butter and salt, stirring it carefully till it boils.

TOMATO SAUCE*
[1862]

Take seven pounds of ripe tomatoes, with the outside skins taken off; put them in a preserving-kettle, with four pounds of sugar, and boil until the sugar penetrates the tomatoes; then add one pint of vinegar, one ounce of cloves, and one ounce of ground cinnamon; boil thirty minutes, then put them up on stone jars and seal up close. They will keep any length of time.

* This sauce is especially good with cold veal or fish.

SALAD DRESSING
[1862]

Rub through a fine sieve a middle-sized mealy potato (boiled) and the yelk of two hard-boiled eggs, both cold. Put this into a basin, with a dessertspoonful* of dry mustard, a saltspoonful of salt, a small quantity of pepper, and a pinch of Cayenne; and mix it well with a wooden spoon. Add to this a fresh egg, well beaten, and a tablespoonful of anchovy sauce, and work the whole together; and then stirring it with the right hand, with the left pour in oil by degrees until it forms a thick paste; now add two teaspoonfuls of common vinegar by degrees, still keeping it stirred, and continue the addition of oil and vinegar in corresponding quantities till, by continued working it forms a stiffish, but perfectly smooth, cream-like sauce. Add a little more anchovy sauce or seasoning, if required; and, if too thick, dilute it by adding a little milk. This dressing will keep some days if no milk is used; or for a small salad half the above quantities will be sufficient.

* 2 teaspoons.

MAYONAISE
[1862]

A fine sauce for eating with cold meat, poultry, fish, or for pouring over salad. Two fresh yolks of unboiled eggs, half a salt spoonful, or rather more, of salt and a little Cayenne, a third of a pint of oil, two tablespoonfuls of vinegar, one tablespoonful of cold water, an onion. Put into a large basin the yolks only of two large, fresh eggs; beat them and strain; add a little salt and Cayenne; stir these well together then add a teaspoonful of salad oil, and work the mixture round with a wooden spoon until it appears like cream; pour in by slow degrees nearly half a pint of oil, continuing at each interval to work the same as at first, until it assumes the smoothness of custard, and not a particle of oil remains visible; then add a couple of tablespoonfuls of plain or tarragon vinegar, and one of cold water to whiten the sauce; a very tiny onion, shaved, finely chopped, and bruised with the point of a knife; add all together.

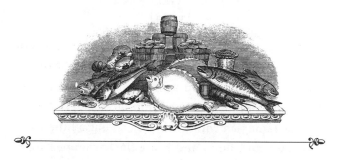

FISH AND SHELLFISH

COLD FISH
[1862]

By the following plan a good dish may be made from any kind of cold fish:* Free the fish from the bone, and cut into small pieces. Season this with onions and parsley chopped, and salt and pepper. Beat two eggs well with a tablespoonful of catsup. Mix the whole together with the fish, and put it in a baking-dish with two or three small slices of bacon over it. Bake before the fire in a Dutch oven. Serve with melted butter or oyster sauce.

* Leftover fish.

To Cook Codfish with
a Piquant Sauce
[1863]

Cut the best part of a codfish in slices, and fry them in butter a light brown color. Take them up out of the pan, and lay them upon a warm dish before the fire. Boil* some onions, cut them into slices, and put them into the same pan with the butter, adding a little vinegar, water, and flour, and some finely-chopped rosemary and parsley. Fry the onions and all the ingredients together, and afterwards pour the whole over the fried fish. This dish will be excellent for three days, as it can be warmed easily when wanted.

* Parboil only one minute.

Fried Eels*
[1867]

Clean and skin the eels; if large, cut them into pieces; if small, skewer them round and fry them whole. First dust them over with yelk of egg and sprinkle them with bread crums. Put them into boiling lard and fry until nicely browned.

* Eels were plentiful and very popular in the United States during the eighteenth and nineteenth centuries.

Fish Fritters
[1865]

Take the remains of any fish which has been served the preceding day, remove all the bones, and pound it in a mortar, add bread crums and mashed potatoes in equal quantities. Mix together half a teacupful of cream, with two well-beaten eggs, some Cayenne pepper and anchovy sauce. Beat all up to a proper consistency, cut it into small cakes, and fry them in boiling lard.

POTTED HERRING
[1861 AND 1862]

Clean the herrings, wash them well, split them open, and boil gently till you can easily pull out the bones; take them out of the water, lay them on a board, pick out the bones, and sprinkle each piece with salt and a little Cayenne pepper. Place in a stone jar a layer of herring, then some grains of allspice, half a dozen cloves, and two or three blades of mace, then another layer of herring, and so on until all are used up. Cover with cold vinegar, tie the jar over closely with thick paper, and set it in a cool oven, to remain there all night. As soon as it becomes cold, the fish are fit for use.

FRIED PERCH
[1863 AND 1866]

Egg and bread-crums, hot lard. Scale and clean the fish, brush it over with egg, and cover with bread-crums. Have ready some boiling lard; put the fish in, and fry a nice brown. Serve with melted butter or anchovy sauce.

To Fry Perch or Tench*
[1863]

Scale and clean them perfectly; dry them well, flour and fry them in boiling lard. Serve plenty of fried parsley round them.

* Tench is a small European freshwater fish.

To Fry Trout
[1862]

Scale, gut and clean them; take out the gills, egg and crumb them; then fry them in lard or oil until of a light brown. Serve with anchovy sauce and sliced lemon.

To Pickle Fish*
[1865]

Take any freshly-caught fish, clean and scale them, wash and wipe dry; cut them into slices a few inches thick, put them in a jar with some salt, some allspice, and a little horseradish; when filled, cover it well with a good cover; let it stand in your oven a few hours; don't let the oven be too hot. This will keep six months. Put it immediately in the cellar, and in a few months they will be fit for use; no bones will be found.

* Before refrigeration fish was often pickled.
In American and English cookbooks of the
eighteenth century there are recipes for
"caveaching" fish in oil, spices, and vinegar.

TO SOUSE ROCK-FISH
[1862]

Boil the fish with a little salt in the water until it is thoroughly cooked. Reserve part of the water in which it was boiled, to which add whole pepper, salt, vinegar, cloves, allspice, and mace, to your taste; boil it up to extract the strength from the spice; and add the vinegar after it is boiled. Cut off the head and tail of the fish and divide the rest in several portions. Put it in a stone jar, and when the fish is quite cold, pour the liquor over it. It will be fit to use in a day or two, and will keep in a cold place two or three weeks.

BAKED SALMON
[1861]

A small salmon may be baked whole. Stuff it with forcemeat made of bread-crumbs, chopped oysters or minced lobster, butter, Cayenne, a little salt, and powdered mace; all mixed well, and moistened with beaten yolk of egg. Bend the salmon round, and put the tail into the mouth, fastening it with a skewer. Put it into a large deep dish; lay bits of butter on it at small intervals,

and set it into the oven.* While baking, look at it occa-sionally, and baste it with the butter. When one side is well browned, turn it carefully in the dish, and add more butter. Bake it till the other side is well browned; then transfer it to another dish with the gravy that is about it, and send it to table.

If you bake salmon in slices, reserve the forcemeat for the outside. Dip each slice first in beaten yolk of egg, and then in the forcemeat till it is well coated. If in one large piece, cover it in the same manner thickly with the seasoning.

The usual sauce for baked salmon is melted butter, flavored with the juice of a lemon and a glass of port wine, stirred in just before the butter is taken from the fire. Serve it up in a sauce-boat.

* Fish is usually baked in a 400° to 450° oven.
Cook until it flakes easily. Do not overcook.

To Boil Salmon
[1862]

Salmon is dressed in various ways, but chiefly boiled in large pieces of a few pounds weight. The middle piece is considered, if not the richest, yet the most sightly; then that adjoining the jowl; the tail part, though near-ly as good, being usually kept for cutlets. It requires great attention, and the boiling must be checked more than once. A piece of four to five pounds will take nearly an hour; but if double that weight, will not require more then twenty minutes beyond that time,

and if crimped, still less will be sufficient; let it, however, boil quickly in the hardest water, on a strainer
placed in a large fish-kettle, and be thoroughly done,
for nothing is more unwholesome and disagreeable
than fish that is undercooked. Skim it well, or the color
will be bad. The moment it is ready lift up the strainer
and rest it across the kettle, that the fish may drain;
cover it with a thick cloth.

TO BAKE A SHAD*
[1862]

Empty and wash the fish with care, but do not open it
more than is necessary, and keep on the head and fins.
Then stuff it with forcemeat. Sew it up, or fasten it with
fine skewers, and rub the fish over with the yolk of egg
and a little of the stuffing.

Put into the pan in which the fish is to be baked,
about a gill of wine, or the same quantity of water
mixed with a tablespoonful of Cayenne vinegar, or
common vinegar will do. Baked in a moderate oven one
and a half or two hours, or according to its size.

* In colonial times it was somewhat disreputable
to eat shad, but Americans acquired a taste for it
after the Revolution.

To Broil Shad
[1862]

This delicate and delicious dish is excellent broiled. Clean, wash, and split the shad, wipe dry and sprinkle it with pepper and salt; broil it like mackerel.*

> * The average shad weighs about 4 pounds,
> which makes about four servings.

Lobster Rissoles
[1868]

Extract the meat of a boiled lobster, mince it as fine as possible, mix with it the coral* pounded smooth, and some yelks of hard boiled eggs pounded also. Season it with Cayenne pepper, powdered mace, and a very little salt. Make a batter of beaten egg, milk and flour. To each egg allow 2 large Tbsp. of milk and a large teaspoonful of flour. Beat the batter well, and then mix the lobster with it gradually, till it is stiff enough to make into oval balls about the size of a large plum. Fry them in the best salad oil, and serve them up either warm or cold. Similar rissoles may be made of raw oysters minced fine, or boiled clams. These should be fried in lard.

> * The unfertilized eggs of the female lobster.

LOBSTER SALAD
[1860]

One large lobster, two dessertspoonfuls of mixed mustard, one gill and a half of vinegar, one gill and a half of sweet oil, the yolks of five hardboiled eggs, salt to the taste, the inside leaves of two cabbage lettuces. Cut the meat and the lettuce in small pieces; boil the eggs hard, and mash with a wooden or silver spoon, with oil enough to make them a smooth paste, then add the vinegar, mustard, pepper, and salt to the taste; mix this dressing thoroughly with the lobster and lettuce, and serve it before the salad becomes flabby.

TO COOK OYSTERS
[1861]

Having selected some oysters of the largest size, drain off the liquor in a fine cloth, and when dry dredge them lightly with flour. Then cut up two or three large onions very small, put in a saucepan a bit of butter, and when it melts throw in your onions. After they have been there two or three minutes add the oysters, and simmer them gently, seasoning with pepper and salt as they are in progress.* When slightly browned, take them off the fire, suffer a few drops of vinegar to moisten them.

* Oysters are usually considered done when they curl
around the edges. Overcooking toughens them.

To Cook Oysters
[1862]

Butter a saucer or shallow dish, and spread over it a layer of crumbled bread, a quarter of an inch thick; shake a little pepper and salt, and then place the oysters on the crumbs; pour over, also, all the liquor that can be saved in opening the oysters; and then fill up the saucer or dish with bread-crumbs, a little more pepper and salt, and a few lumps of butter here and there at the top, and bake half an hour or an hour, according to size. The front of a nice clear fire is the best situation; but if baked in a side oven, the dish should be set for a few minutes in front, to brown the bread.*

* This provides another example of the common use of a large open fireplace for cooking.

Fried Oysters
[1864]

Beat up a couple or three eggs in a cup, and rasp bread crums on a plate with sweet herbs powdered, a lemon-peel. Dry the oysters as much as possible, souse them in the egg, and cover them with crums. Fry them in plenty of good butter.

Oyster Pie
[1863]

Take a large dish, butter it, and spread a rich paste over the sides and round the edge, but not at the bottom.

The oysters should be fresh, and as large and fine as possible. Drain off part of the liquor from the oysters. Put them into a pan, and season them with pepper salt and spice. Stir them well with the seasoning. Have ready the yelks of eggs, chopped fine, and the grated bread. Pour the oysters, with as much of their liquor as you please, into the dish that has the paste* in it. Stew over them the chopped egg and grated bread. Roll out the lid of the pie, and put it on, crimping the edges handsomely. Take a small sheet of paste, cut it into a square, and roll it up. Cut it with a sharp knife into the form of a double tulip. Make a slit in the centre of the upper crust, and stick the tulip in it. Cut out eight large leaves of paste, and lay them on the lid. Bake the pie in a quick oven.

* Use regular pastry for a single-crust meat pie.

SHRIMP PIE
[1860]

Pick a quart of shrimps; if they are very salty season them with only mace and a clove or two. Mince two or three anchovies;* mix these with the spice, and then season the shrimps. Put some butter at the bottom of the dish, and cover the shrimps with a glass of sharp white wine. The paste must be light and thin. They do not take long baking.

* Or substitute 1 teaspoon Worcestershire sauce.

FISH SAUCES

FISH MARINADE
[1861]

[A Court Bouillon]

Marinade is commonly used in France for the purpose of boiling fish, which imbibes from it a more pleasant flavor than it naturally possesses, and has been so generally adopted by English professed cooks that we here insert the receipt: Cut up two carrots, three onions, six shallots, a single clove of garlic, and put them into a stewpan with a piece of butter, a bunch of parsley, and a bundle of sweet herbs; fry the whole for a few minutes, then add very gradually two bottles of any light wine or cider. Put in a handful of salt, two dozen of peppercorns, the same quantity of allspice, and a couple of cloves. Simmer the whole together for one hour and a half, strain the liquor, and put it by for use.

This marinade, if carefully strained after the fish has been taken out, will serve several times for the same purpose, adding a little water each time. Fish dressed in it should simmer very gently, or rather stew than boil, as it affords to mackerel, fresh herrings, perch, roach, and any of the small river fish the advantage of dissolving or so thoroughly softening their bones as to render them more agreeable in eating. For large fish they should be cut into steaks before being marinated. Instead of the wine or cider, a quart of table-beer, a glass of soy, one of essence of anchovies, and one of catsup may be used; or a pint of vinegar and these spices, fennel, chives, thyme, and bay-leaves may be added with the wine, cider, etc. Or, choose a kettle that will suit the size of the fish, into which put two parts water, one of light (not sweet) white wine, a good piece of butter, some stewed onions and carrots, pepper, salt, two or three cloves, and a good bunch of sweet herbs; simmer fifteen minutes, let it become cold, then boil the fish therin. Serve with anchovy sauce and a squeeze of lemon.

FISH SAUCE
[1862 AND 1864]

A pint of port wine,* a quarter of a pint of vinegar, twelve anchovies, a small quantity of pepper, one nutmeg (grated), a few cloves, a quarter of an ounce of mace, a little horseradish and lemon-peel; one onion, a bunch of thyme and parsley. Let all simmer together over a slow fire until the anchovies are dissolved. Strain it through a sieve and bottle it when cold. When you wish the sauce served with the fish to be extremely rich and good, put as much of the above mixture as you would of water into the butter when melting, omitting the water altogether.

* Use either a plain white wine or domestic *white* port.

FISH VINEGAR
[1860]

One ounce and a half of Cayenne pepper, two table-spoonfuls of walnut catsup,* and two tablespoonfuls of sauce,† put into a quart bottle of vinegar, with a few shreds of garlic and shalots. Shake it well every day for a fortnight. Then fill up the bottle with vinegar and it will be fit for use in a few days.

> * A recipe for walnut catsup can be found in
> *Joy of Cooking* (Rombauer and Becker, 1975)
> and other cookbooks.
> †Use soy sauce.

LOBSTER SAUCE
[1862]

Take a large fresh lobster, carefully pick out the berries and all the inside, cut it small; make a sauce with a lump of flour and butter, a little milk or cream, a very small quantity of essence of anchovy,* a very little mace beat fine, and Cayenne, then pull the rest of the lobster to pieces with two forks; add the sauce by degrees to the berries, and put in the lobster. Give it a boil, stirring all the time, and it is ready to serve.

> * Anchovy paste.

POULTRY AND WILDFOWL

CHICKEN BAKED IN RICE
[1861]

Cut a chicken into joints as for a fricassee,* season it well with pepper and salt, lay it into a pudding-dish lined with slices of ham or bacon, add a pint of veal gravy and an onion finely minced; fill up the dish with boiled rice well pressed and piled high as the dish will hold; cover it with a paste of flour and water,† and bake one hour in a slow oven. If you have no veal gravy, use water instead, adding a little more ham and seasoning.

* The chicken pieces should be parboiled.
†Make a regular pot-pie pastry.

To Fricassee Small Chickens
[1868]

Cut off the wings and legs of four chickens, separate the breasts from the backs; divide the backs crosswise; cut off the necks; clean the gizzard; put them with the livers and other parts of the chickens, after being thoroughly washed, into a saucepan; add salt, pepper, and a little mace; cover with water, and stew until tender. Take them up; thicken half a pint of water with two spoonfuls of flour rubbed into four ounces of butter; add a tumbler of new milk; boil all together a few minutes, then add eight spoonfuls of white wine, stirring it in carefully so as not to curdle; put in the chickens, and shake the pan until they are sufficiently heated; then serve them up.

Chicken Salad
[1863]

Boil a chicken that weighs not more than a pound and a half.* When very tender, take it up, cut it in small strips, then take six or seven white heads of celery, scrape, and wash it; cut the white part small, in pieces of about three quarters of an inch long, mix it with the meat of the fowl, and just before the salad is sent in, pour a dressing made in the following way over it:—

Boil four eggs hard; rub their yelks to a smooth paste with two tablespoonfuls of olive oil; two teaspoonfuls of made mustard; one teaspoonful of salt, and one teacupful of strong vinegar.

Place the delicate leaves of the celery around the edges of the dish. White-heart lettuce may be used instead of celery. Any other salad dressing may be used, if preferred.

* Use a regular fryer.
Add green peas with the celery.

CHICKEN PUFFS
[1867]

Mince up together the breast of a chicken, some lean ham, half an anchovy,* a little parsley, some shalot, and lemon-peel, and season these with pepper, salt, Cayenne and beaten† mace. Let this be on the fire a few minutes, in a little good white sauce. Cut some thinly-rolled-out puff paste‡ into squares, putting on each some of the mince, turn the paste over, fry them in boiling lard, and serve them. These puffs are very good cold, and they form a convenient supper dish.

* The anchovy used in this and other recipes
may have been an uncured herring and not
the anchovy we know today; however,
Thomas Jefferson is said to have imported
Mediterranean anchovies from Italy.
†Ground.
‡Puff paste is extra rich and flaky,
especially for dishes such as creamed chicken.

An Egyptian Pillau*
[1862]

Put a good-sized fowl into a pan with some chopped ham, half a pound of sausage meat, some chopped onion, one-quarter of a pound of butter, sweetherbs tied in a bunch, a few dried mushrooms, chopped fine, pepper and salt. Stew the fowl gently until quite tender, adding a little water now and then to prevent it from becoming dry. Pick all the meat from the bones, and cut it into very small pieces, removing the skin. Boil dryly one pound of rice, mix it well with the fowl and gravy, and season it to taste. This must all be finished half an hour before dinner is ready, so that it may be put at the side of the fire and served almost dry; but care must be taken to place it at the side, not on the fire, after it is cooked. This dish is excellent with turkey.

> * "Pillaus," "pilaus," or "pilafs" were typical of Carolina cooking in colonial days. South Carolina produced excellent rice for many years, and many varieties of this dish existed. As this recipe indicates, the secret of all pilaus was to have the exact amount of liquid so the rice turns out dry rather than mushy.

Steamed Fowls
[1868]

Fowls are better steamed than boiled, especially when there is no veal stock on hand to boil them in. When steamed, the juices should be saved by placing a pan under the strainer to catch all the drips. Drawn butter, plain or seasoned with parsley or celery, is the most common sauce for boiled fowls. When oysters can be had, oyster sauce is to be preferred above all others.

To Stew a Duck or Goose
[1860]

Half roast a duck or goose; put it into a stewpan with a pint of beef-gravy, a few leaves of sage and mint cut small, pepper and salt, and a small bit of onion shred as fine as possible; simmer a quarter of an hour,* and skim clean; then add near a quart of green peas; cover close, and simmer near half an hour longer; put in a piece of butter and a little flour, and give it one boil; then serve in one dish.

* Simmer until tender when tested with a fork.

To Roast Turkey
[1860, 1862, 1863, and 1865]

Prepare a stuffing of pork sausage-meat, one beaten egg, and a few crumbs of bread; or, if sausages are to be served with the turkey, stuffing as for fillet of veal; in either, a little shred shallot is an improvement. Stuff the bird under the breast; dredge it with flour, and put it down to a clear, brisk fire; at a moderate distance the first half hour, but afterwards nearer. Baste with butter; and when the turkey is plumped up, and the steam draws towards the fire, it will be nearly done; then dredge it lightly with flour, and baste it with a little more butter, first melted in the basting ladle. Serve with gravy in the dish and bread sauce in the tureen. It may be garnished with sausages, or with fried forcemeat, if veal stuffing be used. Sometimes the gizzard and liver are dipped into the yolk of an egg, sprinkled with salt and Cayenne, and then put under the pinions before the bird is put to the fire. A very large turkey will require three hours roasting*; one of eight or ten pounds, two hours; and a small one, an hour and a half.

* Today's roasting charts call for the following: 8-10 pounds at 325° for 3 to 3½ hours; 10-14 pounds at 325° for 3½ to 4 hours.

To "Devil" Turkey*
[1860]

Mix a little salt, black pepper, and Cayenne, and sprinkle the mixture over the gizzard, rump, and drumstick of a dressed turkey; broil them, and serve very hot with this sauce: mix with some of the gravy out of the dish, a little made mustard, some butter and flour, a spoonful of lemon-juice, and the same of soy; boil up the whole.

* During the eighteenth and nineteenth centuries "deviling" was popular in England and America as a means of dressing up leftover cold meats. Underwood and Co. began canning deviled meats in the 1860s and added deviled turkey in the 1870s. The company's "Red Devil" trademark (1867) is the oldest registered trademark in use in the United States (McIntosh, 1995).

WILD FOWL

WILD DUCKS
[1862]

Wild ducks must be roasted at a very brisk fire; they take from twelve to twenty minutes, according to taste. Some people are of opinion that they should only fly through the kitchen; by epicures they are considered to be in true perfection when they come up dry and brown, and, when cut, flood the dish with gravy. The means of insuring success consists in a very ardent fire, rapid motion of the spit, and constant basting. The carver should score the breast of the duck, put a piece of butter on it, and cut a lemon in half, putting on one half a spoonful of salt, and on the other a spoonful of cayenne; put the two together, and squeeze vigorously over the duck; then pour over them a wine-glass of hot port wine.

TO BROIL PARTRIDGES
[1868]

Split them in half; do not wash them, but wipe their insides with a cloth; dip them into liquid butter, then

roll them in bread-crumbs; repeat this process; lay them inside downwards, upon a well-heated gridiron, turn them but once, and when done serve them with a piquante sauce. If you do not employ butter and bread-crumbs, a little Cayenne and butter should be rubbed upon them before they are served. Cold roasted birds eat well if nicely broiled, and sent to table with a highly seasoned sauce.

To Cook Partridges
[1868]

In making partridges ready for roasting, leave the heads on, and turn them under the left wings; cut off the tops of the toes, but do not remove the legs; before a proper fire, twenty minutes' roasting will be ample for young partridges. After being shot, these birds should not be kept longer than from two days to a week. The plumage is occasionally allowed to remain upon the heads of the red partridges, in which case the heads require to be wrapped in paper.

Partridge Pie
[1868]

Two braces* of partridges are required to make a handsome pie; truss them as for boiling; pound in a mortar the livers of the birds, a quarter of a pound of fat bacon, and some shred parsley; lay part of this forcemeat at the bottom of a raised crust, put in the partridges, add the remainder of the forcemeat and a few mushrooms; put some slices of bacon fat on the top, cover with a lid of crust, and bake it for two hours and a half. Before serving the pie remove the lid, take out the bacon, and add sufficient rich gravy and orange juice. Partridge pie may also be made in a dish in the ordinary way.

* Two braces equal four partridges.

To Fry Partridges
[1868]

Take a brace of cold partridges that have been either roasted or braised; cut them into quarters; dip them into beaten and seasoned yelks of eggs; make some butter or friture* perfectly hot in a frying pan; put into it the birds, and do them over a moderately hot fire until they are beautifully browned.

* Fat or oil for frying.

Pigeon Compote
[1862]

Truss six pigeons* as for boiling; grate the crumb of a small loaf, scrape a pound of fat bacon, chop some thyme, parsley, and onion, and some lemon-peel fine; a little nutmeg, pepper and salt, mix it together with two eggs. Put this forcemeat into the craws[†] of the pigeons, lard the breasts, and fry them brown. Place them in a stewpan, with sufficient beef stock to cover them, and stew them gently three-quarters of an hour; thicken with a piece of butter rolled in flour, serve with force-meat balls round the dish, and strain the gravy over the pigeons.

[*] These were undoubtedly passenger pigeons, at one time so plentiful they blackened the sky when they flew over, but now extinct because of the unlimited hunting of them. This recipe could be used for doves or wood pigeons.
[†] Crops.

PIGEON PIE[*]
[1860]

Rub the pigeons with pepper and salt, inside and out; in the former put a bit of butter, and, if approved, some parsley chopped with the livers and a little of the same seasoning. Lay a beefsteak at the bottom of the dish, and the birds cut in half on it; between every two, a hard egg; put a cup of water in the dish, and, if there is any ham in the house, lay a bit on each pigeon—it is a great improvement to the flavor; season the gizzards and two joints of the wings, and put them in the centre of the pie, and over them, in a hole in the crust, three feet nicely cleaned, to show what pie it is. Cover with puff paste.

[*] Similar recipes, using game birds, can be found in cookbooks today.

WOODCOCK
[1865]

Woodcocks should not be drawn, as the trail* is considered a "bonne bouche;" truss their legs close to the body, and run an iron skewer through each thigh, close to the body, and tie them on a small bird spit; put them to roast at a clear fire; cut as many slices of bread as you have birds, toast or fry them a delicate brown, and lay them in the dripping-pan under the birds to catch the trail; baste them with butter, and froth them with flour; lay the toast on a hot dish, and the birds on the toast; pour some good beef gravy into the dish, and sent some up in a boat; twenty or thirty minutes will roast them. Garnish with slices of lemon.

Snipes differ little from woodcocks, unless in size; they are to be dressed in the same way, but require about five minutes less time to roast them.

* Entrails. The intestines of the woodcock are
especially esteemed and cooked with the bird,
not drawn (see Rombauer and Becker, 1975,
or FitzGibbon, 1976).

SAUCES FOR POULTRY

SAUCE FOR GAME OR POULTRY
[1862]

Put into a stewpan and set on a slow fire a quarter of a pint of white wine, a tablespoonful of vinegar, three tablespoonfuls of olive oil, a bunch of sweet herbs,* and spice to taste. Add to the whole some good gravy, and serve hot.

* For sweet herbs use equal amounts of fresh parsley, tarragon, chives, and chervil, minced.

BREAD SAUCE*
[1864]

For roast turkey, chicken, pheasant, etc. 2 cups of milk; 1 onion; 3 cloves; pinch of mace; 1 cup of bread crumbs; salt and pepper; pinch Cayenne; 2 Tbsp. butter; 1 Tbsp. cream. Put milk in double boiler; put cloves in onion add to milk in double boiler and cook one half hour over boiling water. Strain milk over bread crumbs, add salt and pepper to taste, pinch cayenne, keep warm, add cream just before serving.

* This traditional English thick sauce is still used on game or fowl dishes.

RICE SAUCE
[1865]

[For Chicken or Game]

This is a delicate white sauce for eating with game or chicken, as a change from the usual bread sauce,* and is a good deal used in India. It is very simply made as follows: Soak a quarter of a pound of rice in a pint of milk, with onion, pepper, etc., as for bread sauce.* When it is quite tender, having removed the spice, rub it through a sieve into a clean stew-pan, and boil it. If too thick, add a small quantity of cream or milk.

* See page 148.

STUFFINGS

STUFFING
[1860 AND 1863]

[For Roast Goose]

Peel two onions, cut in half, sprinkle with salt, cover with boiling water and leave for a minute or two, drain and chop small. Cook in two tablespoonsful of butter until tender. Add one half teaspoon of salt; four cups of mashed potato; one half cup of bread crumbs; one teaspoon of rubbed sage; one fourth teaspoon pepper and the yolk of an egg or two. Should stuff a ten to twelve pound goose.

STUFFING
[1860 AND 1865]

[For Turkeys, Fowl, or Veal]

Chop finely, half a pound of suet,* and with it mix the same quantity of bread-crumbs, a large spoonful of chopped parsley, nearly a teaspoonful of thyme and marjoram, mixed; one eighth of a nutmeg, some grated lemon-peel, salt, and pepper; and bind the whole with two eggs. A teaspoonful of finely-shred shallot or onion may be added at pleasure.

> * For suet, substitute desalted
> pork fatback or bulk sausage.

MEATS

BAKED BEEF-STEAK PUDDING*
[1860]

[*Toad-in-a-hole*]

Make a batter of milk, two eggs, and flour; lay a little of it at the bottom of the dish; then put in the steaks, which have been cut in strips and rolled with fat in between, and if shred onion is approved, add a very little, season well with pepper and salt; pour the remainder of the batter over them, and bake it.

---

* According to Weaver's *America Eats,* beef became very popular after the Civil War because of the commercialization of livestock raising. This probably accounts for the number of beef recipes in *Godey's.* Toad-in-the-hole is a traditional English dish.

BEEF COLLOPS
[1863]

Cut the inside of a sirloin, or any other convenient piece, into small circular shapes, flour and fry them, sprinkle with pepper, salt, chopped parsley, and shalot; make a little gravy in the pan; send to table with gherkin or tomato sauce.

—or; cut thin slices of beef from the rump or any other tender part, and divide them into pieces three inches long; beat them with the blade of a knife, and flour them. Fry the collops in butter two minutes; then lay them into a small stewpan, and cover them with a pint of gravy; add a bit of butter rubbed in flour.

BEEFSTEAK PIE
[1860 AND 1863]

Take rump-steaks that have been well hung,* cut in small scallops;† beat them gently with a rolling-pin; season with pepper, salt, and a little shalot minced very fine; put in a layer of sliced potatoes, place the slices in layers with a good piece of fat and a sliced mutton kidney;‡ fill the dish; put some crust on the edge, and about an inch below it, and a cup of water or broth in the dish. Cover with rather thick crust, and set in a moderate oven.

* Aged to make the meat tender.
† Small pieces of about 1½ to 2 inches.
‡ Kidneys need special preparation to remove the core and membrane.

BEEF OLIVES
[1862]

Cut some handsome steaks, flatten them with a roller, dredge them with a small quantity of white pepper and salt, have some forcemeat made with the fat and lean of veal mixed together, a small bit of lean ham or bacon, parsley, and sweet herbs, with a few breadcrums, all beaten in a mortar, and mixed with an egg; lay a little over each steak, and roll it up tightly, fastening with a skewer; dip them in the yolk of an egg, then in crums of bread, and fry them of a pale brown; dish them with brown sauce, in which put a glass of white wine, with some strong gravy, seasoned with Cayenne.

BOEUF AU GRATIN*
[1865]

Most readers know—but there may be one here and there who may like to be reminded—that *au gratin* is a mode of cookery in which the fire is applied above as well as below, the lid of the vessel being formed to hold hot charcoal. Melt some butter at the bottom of the stewpan, add to it fine bread-crums or raspings, and place in a circle thin slices of the beef. Place over them some little pieces of butter, parsley chopped fine, a sprinkle of salt, and a little broth. Let it cook gently, with the fire above and below.

* In America, the term *au gratin* has come
to be associated with a cheese topping,
but the term originally meant
"with the burnt scrapings from the pan."

BOEUF A LA MÉNAGÈRE
[1865]

[Housewife's Beef]

Take about twenty rather small onions, brown them in a frying-pan with a little butter, and when they have taken a bright color, sprinkle over them a little flour or some breadcrums. Remove the onions to a stewpan, taking care not to break them. Add a teacup of broth, the piece of beef whole,* a sufficient seasoning of salt, pepper, and nutmeg, and a bouquet of sweet herbs. Let the whole simmer over a slow fire for about two hours. Serve the beef on a dish, and arrange the onions round it.

* Use a chuck, blade, arm, or crosscut
suitable for a pot roast.

COLLARED BEEF*
[1863]

[Corned Beef]

Choose the thick end of a flank of beef, but do not let it be too fat; let it lie in salt or pickle for a week or ten days. The brisket of beef will also serve for this purpose, from which the bones should be taken, and the inside skin removed. When sufficiently salted, prepare the following seasoning: one handful of parsley, chopped fine, some thyme, marjoram, and basil; season the whole with pepper, and mix all well together, and cover the inside of the beef with it. Roll the meat up tight, then roll it in a clean cloth; bind it with strong string or tape, and tie it close at the ends. Boil it gently from three to four hours, and, when cooked, take it up; tie the ends again quite close to the meat, and place it between two dishes, with a heavy weight at the top. When it is cold remove the cloth.

* An English and Irish method of preparing
an end of a flank of beef.

ENGLISH STEW
[1860 AND 1864]

English stew is the name given to the following excellent preparation of cold meat. Cut the meat in slices; pepper, salt, and flour them, and lay them in a dish. Take a few pickles of any kind, or a small quantity of pickled cabbage,* and sprinkle over the meat. Then take a tea-cup half full of water; add to it a small quantity of the vinegar belonging to the pickles, a small quantity of catsup, if approved of, and any gravy that may be set for use. Stir all together and pour it over the meat. Set the meat before the fire with a tin behind it, or put it in a Dutch oven, or in the oven of the kitchen range, as may be most convenient, for about half an hour before dinnertime. This is a cheap, simple way of dressing cold meat.

* Sauerkraut.

PODOVIES, OR BEEF PATTIES
[1860]

Shred underdone dressed beef* with a little fat, season with pepper, salt, and a little shallot or onion. Make a plain paste,† roll it thin, and cut it in shape like an apple-puff, fill it with the mince, pinch the edges, and fry them of a nice brown. The paste should be made with a small quantity of butter, egg, and milk.

> * Medium-rare beef, with any additional
> seasoning, cut into small cubes.
> †Use an ordinary pastry as you would for a pot pie.
> This recipe could even be made as a pot pie with
> one top crust and baked rather than fried.

SAVORY PIES
[1860]

There are few articles of cookery more generally liked than savory pies, if properly made, and they may be made so of a great variety of things. Some are best eaten when cold, and in that case there should be no suet put into any forcemeat that is used with them. If the pie is either made of meat that will take more dressing, to make it extremely tender, than the baking of the crust will allow, or if it is to be served in an earthen pie-dish, the meat, if beef, must be previously stewed.

A SINEE KABAUB
[1863]

Take a pound weight off a rump of beef, and cut the same into dice-formed pieces, removing all the fat. Have at hand half a dozen races of *green* ginger, a few cloves of fresh garlic, some green shalots and a small portion of green lemon-peel. Take a long, thin iron skewer, cut the ginger into small separate *thin* pieces, serving the

shalots, the garlic, and the lemon-peel after a similar
manner. Then strew a small quantity of fine curry-powder over the meat, and reeve the skewer through one at
a time, intermediately skewering the ginger,
shalots, onions, garlic, and lemon-peel
after the mode following: Meat, shalot,
garlic; meat, ginger, lemon-peel; meat,
shalot, garlic; meat, ginger, lemon-peel, and so on till the
skewers are fully occupied.

Expose the same before a clear, fierce, charcoal fire,
basting the whole with a bunch of fowls' feathers, introduced into fresh *ghee** till done brown. Serve the same
up with boiled rice.

> * To clarify butter or make *ghee:* melt the butter
> over very low heat, remove from fire, and let it
> set for a few minutes allowing the solids to settle.
> Skim the butterfat from the top and strain.
> This produces a clear yellow liquid.

BEEF TONGUE
[1862]

If it has been dried and smoked before it is dressed, it
should be soaked over night, but if only pickled, a few
hours will be sufficient. Put it in a pot of cold water over
a slow fire for an hour or two, before it comes to a boil.
Then let it simmer gently for from three and a half to
four hours, according to its size; ascertain when it is
done by probing it with a skewer. Take the skin off, and
before serving surround the root with a paper frill.

"BUBBLE AND SQUEAK"*
[1865]

Take from a round of beef, which has been well boiled and cold, two or three slices, amounting to about one pound to one and a half pound in weight, two carrots which have been boiled with the joint, in a cold state, as also the hearts of two boiled greens that are cold. Cut the meat into small dice-formed pieces, and chop up the vegetables together; pepper and salt the latter, and fry them with the meat in a pan with a quarter pound of sweet butter; when fully done, add to the pan in which the ingredients are fried, half a gill of fresh catchup, and serve your dish up to the dinner-table with mashed potatoes. The above is an economical and favorite dinner.

* This English dish is at least two hundred years old
and was probably well known in the
nineteenth-century United States.

FRICASSEE OF COLD ROAST BEEF
[1863]

Cut very thin slices of underdone* beef; chop a handful of parsley very small, put it with an onion into a stew-pan, with a piece of butter and a spoonful of flour; let it fry; then add some strong broth; season with salt and

pepper, and simmer very gently a quarter of an hour; then mix into it the yelks of two eggs, a glass of port wine, and a spoonful of vinegar; stir it quickly over the fire a minute or two; put in the beef, make it hot, but do not let it boil; rub the dish with shalot, and turn the fricassee into it.

* Medium-rare.

POTATO PUFFS
[1863]

Take cold roast meat, either beef, mutton, or veal and ham, clear it from gristle, chop small, and season with pepper, salt, and cut pickles. Boil and mash some potatoes, and make them into a paste with one or two eggs, roll it out with a dust of flour, cut it round with a saucer, put some of your seasoned meat on one-half, and fold it over like a puff, prick or nick it neatly round, and fry it a light brown. This is an excellent method of cooking up cold meat.

CANAPES*
[1863]

Cut up an equal quantity of cold roast veal and of sardines in long thin slices, add a fifth of the weight of capers, flavor plentifully with oil, vinegar, and chopped herbs. Serve on pieces of bread about two inches square and half an inch thick, which had been previously fried in butter. Serve cold.

* The use of this term in *Godey's* in 1863 may have been the first time it was seen in print in the United States.

Curry of Veal
[1862]

Cut part of a breast of veal in moderate-sized pieces;
put it in a stewpan with an onion and a shalot sliced
fine, a slice of lemon, one ounce of butter, a little parsley and thyme, and a tablespoon-
ful of curry-powder mixed with
the same quantity of flour, let the
whole sweat together until the meat is
slightly brown;* add sufficient
broth or water for the sauce; let
it boil gently till the veal is done; strain the sauce
through a sieve, pour it over the veal quite hot, and
serve with rice in a separate dish.

> * The method of cooking this veal today
> would be braising.

Harricot of Veal*
[1860]

Take the best end of a small neck; cut the bones short,
but leave it whole; put it into a stew pan, and just cover
with brown gravy; when it is nearly done, have ready a
pint of boiled peas, six cucumbers pared and sliced, and
two cabbage-lettuces cut into quarters, all stewed in a
little good broth; put them to the veal and let them simmer ten minutes. When the veal is in the dish, pour the

sauce and vegetables over it, and lay the lettuce with forcemeat balls around it.

> *A *harricot* is essentially a ragout. It can be traced to
> at least the fourteenth century and was originally
> made with mutton but later with other meat as well.
> It is sometimes spelled *haricot* or *harico*.

VEAL AND OYSTER PIE
[1862 AND 1863]

Make seasoning of pepper, salt, and a small quantity of grated lemon-peel. Cut some veal cutlets, and beat them until they are tender; spread over them a layer of pounded ham, and roll them round; then cover them with oysters, and put another layer of the veal fillets, and oysters on the top. Make a gravy of the bones and trimmings, or with a lump of butter, onion, a little flour and water; stew the oyster liquor, and put to it, and fill up the dish, reserving a portion to put into the pie when it comes from the oven.

RISSABLES*
[1868]

Rissables are made with veal and ham chopped very fine, or pounded lightly; add a few bread crumbs, salt, pepper, nutmeg and a little parsley and lemon-peel; mix all together with the yelks of eggs, well beaten; either roll them into shape like a flat sausage or into the shape of pears, sticking a bit of horseradish in the ends to resemble the stalks; egg each over† and grate bread crumbs; fry them brown, and serve on crisp fried parsley.

* The name is a derivative of the verb *rissoler,*
meaning to brown. A rissole is an entrée made
of meat or fish chopped up and mixed with
bread crumbs and egg, then rolled into a ball
or small cake and fried.
† "Egg over" means to dip in egg
(1 egg, 2 tablespoons water, beaten slightly),
then dip in crumbs before sautéing.

ROLLED VEAL
[1863]

The breast is the best for this purpose. Bone a piece of the breast, and lay forcemeat over it of herbs, bread, an anchovy,* a spoonful or two of scraped ham, a very little mace, white pepper, and chopped chives; then roll, bind it up tight, and stew it in water or weak broth with the bones, some carrots, onions, turnips, and a bay-leaf. Let the color be preserved, and serve it in veal gravy, or fricassee sauce.

* Optional.

SWEETBREAD CUTLETS
[1863]

[*Veal*]

Boil the sweetbreads* for half an hour in water, or veal broth, and when they are perfectly cold,† cut them into slices of equal thickness, brush them with yolks of egg, and dip them into very fine bread-crumbs, seasoned with salt, Cayenne, grated lemon-rind, and mace; fry them in butter of a fine light brown, arrange them in a dish, placing them high in the centre, and pour under them a gravy made in the pan, thickened with mushroom powder, and flavored with lemon-juice; or, in lieu of this, sauce them with some rich brown gravy, to which a glass of sherry or Madiera has been added.

* The thymus gland of a young animal.
†The membrane should be removed at this point.

Scallops of Cold Veal
[1861]

Mince the meat extremely small, and set it over the fire with a scrape of nutmeg, a little pepper and salt, and a little cream, for a few minutes; then put it into the scallop-shells,* and cover them with crumbs of bread, over which put some bits of butter, and brown them before the fire.

Either veal or chicken looks and eats well prepared in this way, and lightly covered with crumbs of bread fried; or these may be put on in little heaps.

* Or ramekins.

Broiled Kidneys
[1860]

[Lamb]

Kidneys* should be split open, scored, and peppered, as well as salted. They are then kept open by a fine iron skewer, and placed flat upon the gridiron, after which they are soon done. They require no gravy or garnish.

* The core and membrane should be removed.

LAMB CHOPS [BRAISED]
[1869]

Fry them a light brown, in butter, then add a little water, flour, salt and a dust of pepper, to the gravy; let it brown, and pour it over the chops.

BROILED LAMB STEAK
[1869]

Broil slowly until quite done, then make a gravy with fresh butter melted by the steak, add a dust of pepper, and a little salt dissolved in a tablespoonful of water; serve with peas, potatoes, and salads.*

* Lamb dishes are traditionally served with
mint sauce (page 177) or mint jelly.

LAMB CUTLETS
[1864]

[A French Dish]

Cut a loin of lamb into chops. Remove all the fat, trim them nicely, scrape the bone, and see that it is the same length in all the cutlets. Lay them in a deep dish and cover them with salad oil. Let them steep in the oil for an hour. Mix together a sufficiency of finely grated bread crumbs, and a little minced parsley, seasoned with a very little pepper and salt and some grated nutmeg. Having drained the cutlets from the oil, cover them with the mixture, and broil them over a bed of hot, live coals, on a previously heated gridiron, the bars of which have been rubbed with chalk.* The cutlets must be thoroughly cooked. When half done, turn them carefully. You may bake them in a Dutch oven instead of broiling them. Have ready some boiled potatoes, mashed smooth and stiff with cream or butter. Heap the mashed potatoes high on a heated dish and make it into the form of a dome or bee-hive. Smooth it over with the back of a spoon, and place the lamb cutlets all round it, so that they stand up and lean against it, with the broad end of each cutlet downward. In the top of the dome of potatoes stick a handsome bunch of curled parsley.

* This procedure is not necessary today; preheat and rub with a piece of fat from the meat.

ROAST LEG OF LAMB
[1860 AND 1865]

Make deep incisions round the bone and in the flesh, prepare a dressing of breadcrumbs, salt, pepper, sweet marjoram, or savory, and as much butter as will make the crumbs adhere together; fill all the incisions with the dressing; season the meat with salt and pepper; roast

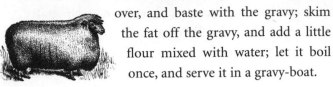

it before a clear fire, and when nearly done, dredge flour over, and baste with the gravy; skim the fat off the gravy, and add a little flour mixed with water; let it boil once, and serve it in a gravy-boat.

An Irish Stew*
[1861]

Cut six rather thick chops from the loin; when the square ends of the bones are cut off, these will probably weigh two pounds; lay them in an iron pot, and put four pounds of sliced potatoes, placed in layers, with the chops, and half a dozen small onions, with about a quart of water; cover the pan closely and let them stew on a moderate fire for two hours, or until the potatoes have become nearly a mash, and absorbed all the water and gravy of the meat; the chops will then be found very tender, and the potatoes rich with the fat. The stew should be eaten hot, but without any kind of sauce.

* A traditional version of the classic Irish dish.
Sauté the onions first. Degrease the liquid. The
addition of a bay leaf, 2 tablespoons chopped parsley,
and a bit of marjoram makes it more palatable.

To Broil, or Fry Pork Cutlets
[1862 and 1865]

[Or Pork Chops]

Cut them about half an inch thick from a delicate loin of pork, trim them into neat form, and take off part of the fat or the whole of it when it is not liked; dredge a little pepper or Cayenne upon them, and broil them over a clear and moderate fire from fifteen to eighteen minutes, sprinkle a little fine salt upon them just before they are dished. They may be dipped into egg and then into bread crums mixed with minced sage, then finished the usual way. When fried, flour them well, and season them with salt and pepper first. Serve them with gravy made in the pan, or with sauce.

BROILED PORK STEAK
[1869]

The tenderloin is the best for steak, but any lean white meat is good. Broil slowly, after splitting it so as to allow it to cook through without drying or burning. When ready to turn over dip the cooked side in a nice gravy or butter, pepper and salt, which should be prepared on a platter and kept hot without oiling. It must be well done; there should be no sign of blood in the meat when cut. It requires slow broiling; it will take at least 20 minutes to broil a pork-steak.

PORK AND APPLE FRITTERS
[1867]

Prepare a light batter, freshen* or use cold boiled or baked pork. Cut it fine enough for hash, and fry it a little to extract some of the fat for frying the fritters. Peel sour apples, and cut or chop them quite as fine as the pork; mix first the pork and then the apples in the batter, and fry them brown.

Potatoes, parsnips, salsify, or any vegetable desired, can be used in the same manner.†

* Serve with Piquante Sauce, page 179.
† "Freshen" refers to salt pork placed in
cold water and simmered. Repeat as necessary.

To Roast a Leg of Pork
[1865]

[Fresh Ham]

Cut a slit near the knuckle, and fill the space with sage and onion, chopped fine and seasoned with pepper and salt, with or without bread crumbs. Rub sweet oil* on the skin, to prevent it blistering and make the crackling crisp; and the outer rind may be scored with lines, about half an inch apart. If the leg weighs seven or eight pounds, it will require from two and a half to three hours roasting before a strong fire. Serve with applesauce and potatoes; which are likewise eaten with all joints of roasted pork.

If the stuffing be liked mild, scald the onions before chopping them. If pork is not stuffed, you may serve it

up with sage and onion sauce, as well as apple-sauce which should always accompany roast pork, whether it be stuffed or not; and also with mustard.

* Substitute salad oil.

BACON ROLL PUDDING
[1864]

Boil a pound of fat bacon for half an hour, and then cut it up into slices. Peel six apples and one onion, and cut them in slices. Make two pounds of flour into a stiff dough, roll it out thin; first lay the slices of bacon out all over this, and then upon the slices of bacon spread out the slices of apples and the slices of onion; roll up the paste so as to secure the bacon, etc., in it; place the bolster pudding in a cloth, tied at each end, and let it boil for two hours in a two-gallon pot, with plenty of water.

SNITZ AND KNEP*
[1866]

Take of sweet dried apples (dried with the skins on if you can get them) about one quart. Put them in the bottom of a porcelain or tin-lined boiler with a cover. Take a nice piece of smoked ham washed very clean, and lay on top; add enough water to cook them nicely. About twenty minutes before dishing up, add the following dumplings.

Dumplings: Mix a cup of warm milk with one egg, a little salt, and a little yeast, and enough flour to make a sponge. When light, work into a loaf. Let stand until about twenty minutes before dinner, then cut off slices or lumps, and lay on the apples, and let steam through.

* Now known as "Schnitz-un-Gnepp" or dried apples and dumplings, this is an old Pennsylvania Dutch dish, originally made without meat.

FRENCH RECEIPT FOR BOILING A HAM
[1862]

After having soaked, thoroughly cleaned, and trimmed the ham, put over it a little, very sweet, clean hay, and tie it up in a thin cloth; place it in a ham kettle, a braising pan, or any other vessel as nearly of its size as can be, and cover it with two parts of cold water, and one of light, white wine (we think the reader will perhaps find *cider* a good substitute for this); add, when it boils and has been skimmed, four or five carrots, two or three onions, a large bunch of savory herbs* and the smallest bit of garlic. Let the whole simmer gently from four to five hours or longer should the ham be very large. When perfectly tender, lift it out, take off the rind, and sprinkle over it some fine crums, or some raspings of bread mixed with a little finely minced parsley.

* Equal parts parsley, bay leaf, and thyme.

WESTPHALIA HAMS*
[1860]

Prepare the hams in the usual manner by rubbing them with common salt and draining them; take one ounce of saltpetre, one-half pound of coarse sugar, and the same quantity of salt; rub it well into the ham, and in three days pour a pint of vinegar over it. A fine foreign flavor may also be given to hams by pouring old strong beer over them and burning juniper wood while they are drying; molasses, juniperberries and highly-flavored herbs, such as basil, sage, bay-leaves, and thyme, mingled together, and the hams well rubbed with it, using only a sufficient quantity of salt to assist in the cure, will afford an agreeable variety.

* Westphalia was a former Prussian province of western Germany (part of the British zone of occupation in 1946) and was famous for its hams. This recipe was undoubtedly furnished by German American immigrants. These hams are usually soaked in brine for four weeks, smoked slowly over a hickory fire, covered with ground black pepper, and hung in a dry place for several months.

HAM TOAST
[1860 AND 1863]

Melt a small piece of butter in a stewpan until it is slightly browned; beat up one egg and add it to it; put in as much finely minced ham as would cover a round of buttered toast, adding as much gravy as will make it moist when quite hot. When all the ingredients are in, stir them quickly with a fork; pour onto the buttered toast, which cut in pieces afterwards any shape you please. Serve hot.

SAUSAGE CAKES
[1865]

Chop a pound of good pork, fine; add half a teaspoonful of pepper, half a spoonful of cloves, half a spoonful of coriander seed,* and four tablespoonfuls of cold water. Mix all well together, form them into small cakes, and fry in a hot pan.

* Or 1 teaspoon sage, ½ teaspoon salt.
Use two-thirds lean meat and one-third fat.

A CURRY OF MEAT OR RABBIT
[1861]

Cut six onions in very thin rings, fry them in butter till quite brown; put them in a warm stew-pan. Cut the meat, or rabbit or poultry in small joints, fry it brown, but quickly; put it on the onions; mix a tablespoonful of curry powder with a teaspoonful of flour and a teaspoonful of salt, a quarter of a pint of vinegar, and a quarter of a pint of port wine; mix all thoroughly and smoothly, and pour it over the meat, then stew very slowly for one hour; dish it up with rice round it.

RABBIT SOUP*
[1861]

Begin this soup six hours before dinner. Cut up three large but young and tender rabbits, or four small ones (scoring the backs) and dredge them with flour. Slice six mild onions, and season them with half a grated nutmeg, or more, if you like it. Put some fresh butter into a hot frying-pan (you may substitute for the butter some cold roast-veal gravy that has been carefully cleared from the fat), place it over the fire, and when it boils, put in the rabbits and onions, and fry them of a light brown. Then transfer the whole to a soup-pot; season it with a very small teaspoonful of salt, a teaspoonful of whole pepper, a large teaspoonful of sweet marjoram leaves stripped from the stalks, and four or five blades of mace, adding three large carrots in slices. Pour on, slowly, four quarts of hot water† from a kettle already boiling hard. Cover the soup-pot, and let it simmer slowly, skimming it well, till the meat of the rabbits is reduced to shreds and drops from the bones, which will not be in less than five hours, if boiled as gently as it ought. When quite done, strain the soup into a tureen. Have ready the grated yolks of six hard boiled eggs, and stir them into the soup immediately after it is strained and while it is very hot. Add, also, some bread cut into dice or small squares, and fried brown or fresh buttered toast, with all the crust removed, and cut into very small bits or mouthfuls.

* Otherwise known as rabbit stew, this was a traditional English country dish.
†If the amount of water is reduced to 2 quarts and simmered about 2 hours, or until tender, it will be more like a stew.

VENISON PASTY
[1860]

A shoulder boned makes a good pasty, but it must be beaten and seasoned, and the want of fat supplied by that of a fine well-hung loin of mutton, steeped twenty-four hours in equal parts of rape vinegar, and port. The shoulder being sinewy, it will be of advantage to rub it well with sugar for two or three days, and when to be used wipe it perfectly clean from it and the wine.

To prepare venison for pasty—Take the bones out, then season and beat the meat; lay it into a stone jar in large pieces pour upon it some plain drawn-beef gravy,* but not a strong one; lay the bones on the top, then set the jar in a saucepan of water over the fire, simmer three or four hours, then leave it in a cold place till next day. Remove the cake of fat, lay the meat in handsome pieces on the dish; if not sufficiently seasoned, add more pepper, salt or pimento, as necessary. Put some of the gravy *[sic]*, and keep the remainder for the time of serving. If the venison be thus prepared, it will not require so much time to bake, or such a very thick crust as is usual, and by which the under part is seldom done through. A mistake used to prevail that venison could not be baked too much; but, as above directed, three or four hours in a slow oven will be quite sufficient to make it tender, and the flavor will be preserved. Either in a shoulder or side, the meat must be cut in pieces, and laid with fat between, that it may be proportioned to each person without breaking up the pasty to find it. Lay some pepper and salt at the bottom of the dish, and some butter; then the meat nicely packed, that it may be sufficiently done, but not lie hollow to harden at the edges. The venison bones should be boiled with some fine old mutton; of this gravy put half a pint cold into the dish, then lay butter on the venison, and cover as well as line the sides of the dish with a thick crust of puff paste, but do not put one under the meat. Keep the remainder of the gravy till the pasty comes from the oven; put it into the middle by a funnel, quite hot, and shake the dish to mix well. It should be seasoned with salt and pepper.

* Probably clear beef broth without added seasoning.

STUFFING AND FORCEMEAT

FORCEMEAT
[1867]

Half a pound of bread-crumbs, a tablespoonful of finely chopped parsley, a tsp. of sweet herbs,* a little grated nutmeg, and lemon-peel; seasoning of salt, pepper and Cayenne; two ounces of beef suet, very finely chopped, and two eggs a little beaten. Mix all together. The flavor of a little chopped lean ham is relished by some persons.

* For sweet herbs, use equal amounts of fresh parsley,
tarragon, chives, and chervil, minced.

STUFFING FOR ROAST VEAL
[1860 AND 1864]

Four cups of dried bread-crumbs, one cup of chopped suet, one cup of chopped onion and one cup of chopped celery, one fourth teaspoon each, thyme, marjoram, savory, pepper and one teaspoon salt, two eggs slightly beaten. Mix thoroughly and stuff into pocket.

MEAT SAUCES

MOCK CAPER SAUCE
[1863]

Cut some pickled green peas, French beans, gherkins, or nasturtiums, into bits the size of capers; put them into half a pint of melted butter, with two teaspoonfuls of lemon-juice, or nice vinegar.

GREEN MINT SAUCE
[1864]

The mint for this sauce should be fresh and young, for the leaves when old are tough. Strip them from the stems, wash them with great nicety, and drain them on a sieve or dry them in a cloth. Chop them very fine, put them into a sauce-tureen, and to three heaped table-spoonsful of the mint add two of pounded sugar; mix them well, and then add gradually six tablespoonsful of good vinegar. The sauce made thus is excellent but

Lisbon sugar* can be used for it when preferred, and all the proportions can be varied to the taste. It is commonly served too liquid, and not sufficiently sweetened; and it will be found much more wholesome, and generally for more palatable made by this receipt.

* Use fine fruit sugar.
This sauce is used with lamb dishes.

HORSE-RADISH SAUCE*
[1865]

This delicious sauce, a great improvement upon the plainly scraped horse-radish for eating with either hot or cold roast beef, is made as follows; A dessertspoon of olive oil or cream the same quantity of powdered mustard, a tablespoonful of vinegar, and two tablespoonfuls of scraped horse-radish, with a little salt to taste, must be stirred and beaten up together until thoroughly well mixed. Serve the sauce separately in a sauce tureen. It will keep for two or three days, or even longer if oil and not cream be used.

* This is more of a relish than a sauce. It is very strong. Today it would be simple to put the roots in a food processor or blender. It would keep much longer than two or three days if refrigerated. Of course, cooks did not have pasteurized cream then either. This would be an excellent accompaniment to ham and to smoked fish.

SAUCE FOR ROAST BEEF OR MUTTON*
[1863]

Grate horse-radish on a bread-grater into a basin; then add two tablespoonfuls of cream, with a little mustard and salt; mix them well together; then add four tablespoonfuls of the best vinegar, and mix the whole thoroughly. The vinegar and cream are both to be cold; add a little powdered white sugar. This is a very fine sauce; it may be served in a small tureen.

* This is a very hot sauce!

A SAUCE PIQUANTE
[1862]

Put into a saucepan a wineglass of vinegar, some thyme, a laurel leaf,* garlic, shallots, and some pepper. Put it on the fire until it is reduced to half the quantity. Add to it some bouillon, gravy or soup, whatever you may have at hand. Pass it through a sieve, rub some butter into a little flour and add it to the sauce, with herbs chopped finely. This makes a good sauce *piquante* for cutlets or warmed slices of meat as well as for tongues.

* Or a bay leaf.

THICKENING
[1863]

Clarified butter is best for this purpose; but if you have none ready, put some fresh butter into a stewpan over a slow, clear fire, when it is melted, add fine flour sufficient to make it the thickness of paste; stir it well together with a wooden spoon for fifteen or twenty minutes, till it is quite smooth: this must be done very gradually and patiently; if you put it over too fierce a fire to hurry it, it will become bitter and empyreumatic: pour it into an earthen pan, and keep it for use. It will keep good a fortnight in summer, and longer in winter.

PASTRIES AND PIES

PASTRY
[1868]

In making pastry the cook should be particularly clean and neat. Her utensils should be kept in order, and when they are done with they should be carefully cleaned and put in their places. Her pasteboard and rolling pin, let it be remembered, should after using, be well scoured with hot water alone. She should not use soap or sand. A marble slab is preferable to a board for rolling paste. Both are generally made too small to be convenient. Three feet long by two feet wide is a good size. In making a paste a good cook will have no waste of any kind, and particularly she will not make more at one time than she wants, under the idea that she can keep it in flour till the next time of making; for it is ten to one that the old paste will spoil the new. No flour except the very best can be used for fine descriptions of pastry, and in damp weather it should be dried before the fire but not scorched. Clarified dripping, good lard, marrow, salt butter, well washed, may be used for ordinary pastry; indeed, if they are pure and sweet they will form good pastry, with good flour and management. In wealthy families, however, where economy is not an object, and everything for the table is required to be of the first quality, the safest plan is to use the best fresh butter. The fat that settles on stews, and on the broth in which meat has been boiled, may be used for pastry, that is, provided it is tasteless. Suet is sometimes used for meat pies, but though it makes a light crust, when hot, it does not eat well when cold.

A great deal more butter, or fat or some kind or other, was formerly directed to be used in making pastry than at present. For ordinary purposes, half the weight of lard or butter is sufficient, but in the richest crusts the quantity should never exceed the weight of flour. Eggs may be added to enrich the crust. Use no more water or other liquid in making paste than is absolutely necessary, or, in other words, take care not to "put out the miller's eye," that is, to make the paste too moist. The great thing is to incorporate the flour well with the fat, which you cannot do if you allow too much water or milk in the first instance.

The under or side crust, which should be thin, should not be made so rich as the top crust, as otherwise it will make the gravy or syrup greasy. All dishes in which pies are to be baked should be buttered or greased round the edges to prevent the crust from sticking, and if there be an under crust, all over the inside, and the same must be done with tins or saucers. Fruit pies or large tarts should have a hole made in the middle of the crust.

PIE-CRUST—FOR MEAT PIES
[1865]

Take one pound of dried flour and rub into it six ounces of lard, six ounces of butter, a small quantity of salt, and a half teaspoonful of baking powder. Mix all these ingredients well together, and then use as much water as will make them into a nice stiff paste. Roll it out, let it stand for about ten minutes and then roll it once more before putting it on the meat. The pie should be baked in a moderately quick oven.

RICH SHORT CRUST
[1860]

To half a pound of flour put not quite half a pound of butter, two ounces of finely-sifted sugar, and the yolk of an egg beat up with a tablespoonful of water. The butter, sugar, and flour to be well mixed before the fire, then add the egg and water.

PIE CRUST—FOR FRUIT PIES
[1865]

Take one pound of dried flour, and one pound of butter, well squeezed in a clean cloth, to get the salt out.

Break the butter with your fingers amongst the flour, as fine as possible, and then with a little cold water mix into a tolerably stiff paste. Gently roll it, passing the roller in one direction only—from you. After this lightly fold it over, and set it aside for a quarter of an hour in a cool place; then repeat the rolling in the same manner, and let it stand another quarter of an hour. This is to be repeated once more. Be sure to handle it as little as possible, and to keep it cool. Bake in a quick oven.

PUFF PASTE
[1868]

[Extra Rich and Flaky]

This paste is nearly the same as what we have called flaky crust, and of course made upon the same principles. If eggs are desired, allow three yelks to a pound of butter or lard. Rub a fourth part of the fat to a cream, then mix the eggs with it, and afterwards the flour. A very little water will suffice to wet it. Beat it with the pin to make it flaky; roll it out thin three times, putting in a portion of the fat each time, and roll it from you; after each rolling beat it well.

RAISED CRUST* [FOR PORK PIE]
[1868]

Put two pounds and a half of flour on the paste-board, and put on the fire in a saucepan three quarters of a pint of water and half a pound of good lard; when the water boils make a hole in the middle of the flour, pour in the water and lard by degrees, gently mix it with a spoon, and when it is well mixed, then knead it with your hands till it becomes stiff; dredge a little flour to prevent it sticking to the board, or you cannot make it smooth; then set it aside for an hour, and keep it cool; do not roll it with your rolling-pin, but roll it with your hands, about the thickness of a quart pot; cut it into six pieces, leaving a little for the covers; put the left hand, clenched, in the middle of one of the pieces, and with the other on the outside, work it up against the back of the left to a round or oval shape. It is now ready for the meat, which must be cut into small pieces with some fat, and pressed into the pie; then cover it with the paste previously rolled out to a proper thickness, and of the size of the pie; put this lid on the pie and press it together with your thumb and finger, cut it all around with a pair of scissors, and bake for an hour and a half. Our good old country housewives pride themselves very much upon being able to raise a large and high pork pie. This crust will answer for many meat and other pies baked in dishes or tins.

> * "Meat or game completely enclosed in pastry is known as a raised pie. Special moulds and a special pastry called hot water crust are used for this type of pie. In Britain the most famous raised pies are pork pie, and veal and ham pie" (FitzGibbon, 1976: 337).

Baked Custard [Pie]
[1861]

Mix a quart of new milk with eight well-beaten eggs, strain the mixture through a fine sieve, and sweeten it with from five to eight ounces of sugar, according to taste; add a small pinch of salt, and pour the custard into a deep dish, with or without a lining or rim of paste, grate nutmeg or lemon rind over the top, and bake it in a very slow oven.

Boston Cream Cakes
[1862]

[Cream Puffs—Paste and Filling]

Take a quart of new milk, and set it on the fire to boil. Moisten four tablespoonfuls of sifted flour with three tablespoonfuls of cold milk. Separate four eggs and beat them up well; add to the yelks five *heaping* tablespoonfuls of sifted loaf-sugar; when the milk is hot—on the point of boiling—stir in the moistened flour; let it thicken, but not boil. Now stir up the whites and yelks of the eggs together; beat them up and stir to them a little of the hot milk, and then stir them into the whole quart of milk. Let it boil for three minutes, add the grated rind and the juice of one lemon to it, and set it away to cool. You must now proceed to make the paste. Take a pint of sifted flour and a quarter of a pound of butter (fresh, of course); place it over hot water till the butter melts, add a quart of milk, and stir in three-fourths of a pound of flour (that is your pint of flour). Let it scald through and become cold before you beat all the lumps out into a paste; separate twelve eggs*, beat them, and stir in (first the yelks, and then the whites) to the paste. Butter twenty-four round in pans, line and cover with this paste, bake thoroughly; when cold, lift the lid, and fill up with your cream; put the edges together, and wet them with a little egg. They should be eaten the day they are made.

* This recipe illustrates how plentiful eggs
were in the mid-1800s.

CHEESECAKES
[1863]

Two ounces of sweet almonds, a little better than an ounce of bitter do,* the whites of two eggs, a quarter of a pound of lump-sugar pounded very fine. Pound up the almonds (after blanching them); mix in the whites of the eggs with the sugar, and bake until a light brown in patty pans† lined with a paste.

* See "Bitter Almond" in Glossary.
† Small round tart pans, plain or fluted.

Lemon Cheesecakes*
[1862 and 1863]

One pound of loaf sugar, six eggs, but the whites of four only, the juice of three large lemons, but first, before cutting them, rub the sugar on the rinds to extract the flavor. Beat the eggs well; add them to the juice of the lemons; then strain them into a bright tin saucepan; add a quarter of a pound of *fresh* butter and all the other ingredients. Let it simmer slowly over a slow fire till the whole is the consistence of honey; stir the mixture till cool, when, after having lined the patty-pans with puff paste, bake them, then put on the lemon mixture, and return them to the oven a few minutes just to very slightly brown over.

> * In earlier times, "cheesecake" referred to any
> open tart made with eggs and lemon or
> orange juice (see FitzGibbon, 1976: 91).

Cocoanut Pie
[1861]

Cut off the brown part of the cocoanut, grate the white part, and mix it with milk, and set it on the fire, and let it boil slowly eight or ten minutes. To a pound of the grated cocoanut allow a quart of milk, eight eggs, four tablespoonfuls of sifted white sugar, a glass of wine,* a small cracker pounded fine, two spoonfuls of melted butter, and half a nutmeg. The eggs and sugar should be beaten together to a froth, then the wine stirred in. Put them into the milk and cocoanut, which should be first allowed to get quite cool, add the cracker and nutmeg, turn the whole into deep pie-plates, with a lining and rim of puff paste. Bake them as soon as turned into the plates.

* Sweet sherry or port.

CRANBERRY TART*
[1861 AND 1869]

Take half a pint of cranberries, pick them from the stems, and throw them into a saucepan with half a pound of white sugar and a spoonful of water; let them come to a boil, peel and cut up four large apples, put a rim of light paste round your dish, strew in the apples, pour the cranberries over them, cover with a lid of crust, and bake for an hour. For a pudding, proceed in the same manner with the fruit, and boil it in the basin or cloth.

* *Tart* usually means a dessert pie.

GREEN APPLE PIES
[1862]

Grate raw six good apples, add a cup of sugar, three tablespoonfuls of melted butter, four eggs,* a little lemon-juice, two tablespoonfuls of brandy, a few dried

currants, and a little spice. Line plates with a paste,† fill
and bake without an upper crust.

* Slightly beaten.
† Pie crust dough.

LEMON PIE
[1863]

Take four lemons, grate the rind, squeeze the juice, chop
the pulp very fine, four teacups of sugar, the yelks of six
eggs, two teacups of milk, four tablespoonfuls of cornstarch; beat well together and bake;* beat the whites of
the eggs with six tablespoonfuls of white sugar to a
froth; when the pies are baked, put the froth† over them,
and set them in the oven for five minutes.

* Bake in a pie crust.
† Meringue.

MINCEMEAT [PIE]
[1861 AND 1862]

Six pounds of currants, three pounds of raisins stoned,
three pounds of apples chopped fine, four pounds of
suet, two pounds of sugar, two pounds of beef, the peel
and juice of two lemons, a pint of sweet wine, a quarter
of a pint of brandy, half an ounce of mixed spice. Press
the whole into a deep pan when well mixed.

Another way.—Two pounds of raisins, three
pounds of currants, three pounds of beef-suet, two

pounds of moist sugar, two ounces of citron, one ounce of orange-peel, one small nutmeg, one pottle of apples chopped fine, the rind of two lemons and juice of one, half a pint of brandy; mix well together. This should be made a little time before wanted for use.

MINCEMEAT WITHOUT MEAT
[1864]

One pound hard apples cut small, one pound currants, half a pound shred raisins, half a pound beef suet, quarter of a pound moist sugar, one ounce lemon and citron-peel, quarter of an ounce cinnamon, one drachm* mace, the rind of a lemon grated, one glass of brandy, and two glasses of sherry. Double the above for large families.

* A drachm (dram) is a metric *fluid* measure.

MOLASSES PIE*
[1862, 1863, AND 1865]

Four eggs—beat the whites separate—one teacupful of brown sugar, half a nutmeg, two tablespoonfuls of butter, beat them well together; stir in one teacupful and a half of molasses, and then add the white of eggs. Bake on pastry.†

* Although probably from the South, this pie may be
an ancestor of shoo-fly pie, a dessert often attributed
to the Pennsylvania Dutch.
† As for a one-crust pie.

OPEN GERMAN TART
[1863]

Half a pound of flour, quarter of a pound butter, quarter of a pound of sugar, and one egg, to be rolled out and baked on a flat surface, having first covered the top with slices of apples or plums.*

A round shape looks best, with a little rim of the paste round the edge.†

* Plus sugar and a dribble of lemon juice.
† As for a one-crust pie.

PUMPKIN PIE
[1860 AND 1861]

Take out the seeds, and pare the pumpkin or squash; but in taking out the seeds do not scrape the inside of the pumpkin; the part nearest the seed is the sweetest; then stew the pumpkin, and strain it through a sieve or colander. To a quart of milk for a family pie three eggs are sufficient. Stir in the stewed pumpkin with your milk and beaten-up eggs till it is as thick as you can stir round rapidly and easily. If the pie is wanted richer, make it thinner, and add sweet cream or another egg or two; but even one egg to a quart of milk makes "very decent pies." Sweeten with molasses or sugar; add two teaspoonfuls of salt, two tablespoonfuls of sifted cinnamon, and one of powdered ginger; but allspice may be used, or any other spice that may be preferred. The peel of lemon grated in gives it a pleasant flavor. The more egg, says an American authority, the better the pie. Some put one egg to a gill of milk. Bake about an hour in deep plates or shallow dishes, without an upper crust, in a hot oven.

Sweet Potato Pudding [Pie]
[1861]

Beat to a cream one pound of sugar and one pound of butter; boil and pound fine two pounds of potatoes;* beat the potato by degree into the butter and sugar; add five eggs beaten light, one wineglass of wine, one of brandy, and one of rose-water;† two teaspoonfuls of spice, and half a pint of cream.

Bake it in a crust. This will fill seven puddings.

* This recipe probably does *not* use sweet potatoes but white potatoes and would make several one-crust pies.
† Rosewater is a delicate flavoring that can be found in specialty stores.

CAKES
AND ICINGS

CAKES

[Directions for Large Cakes]

In making cakes it is indispensably necessary that all the ingredients should be heated* before they are mixed; for this purpose everything should be prepared an hour before the time it is wanted, and placed near the fire or upon a stove—the flour thoroughly dried and warmed; the currants, sugar, caraway seeds, and anything else required heated in the same way; butter and eggs should be beaten in basins fitted into kettles or pans of warm water, which will give them the requisite degree of temperature. Without these precautions cakes will be heavy, and the best materials, with the greatest pains, will fail to produce the desired results. The following directions should also be strictly attended to: Currants should be very nicely washed, dried in a cloth, and then set before the fire.[†] Before they are used a dust of dry flour should be thrown among them, and a shake given to them, which causes the cakes to be lighter. Eggs should be very long beaten, whites and yelks apart, and always strained.[‡] Sugar should be pounded in a mortar[§] or rubbed to a powder on a clean board, and sifted through a very fine hair or lawn sieve. Lemon-peel should be pared very thin, and with a little sugar, beaten in a marble mortar to a paste, and then mixed with a little wine or cream, so as to divide easily among the other ingredients. The pans should be of earthenware; nor should eggs, or butter and sugar be beaten in tins, as the coldness of the metal will prevent them from becoming light. Use no flour but the best superfine, for if the flour be of inferior quality, the cakes will be heavy, ill-colored and unfit to eat; but if a little potato flour be added, it will improve their lightness. Cakes are frequently rendered hard, heavy, and uneatable by misplaced economy in eggs and butter, or for want of a due seasoning in spices and sugar. After all the articles are put into the pan they should be thoroughly and long beaten, as the lightness of the cake depends much on their being well incorporated. Unless you are provided with proper utensils as well as materials the difficulty of making cakes will be so great as in most instances to be a failure. Accuracy in proportioning the ingredients is also indispensable, and therefore scales, weights, and measures, down to the smallest quantity, are of the utmost importance. When yeast is used, a cake should stand for some time to rise before it is put into the oven. All stiff cakes should be beaten with the hand; but pound and similar cakes should be beaten with a whisk or spoon.

* Warmed to room temperature.
†This procedure for currants serves the
same purpose as plumping them.
‡To keep the germ and pieces of shell out.
§Use powdered (regular) or "instant"
(quick dissolving) sugar.

CHRISTENING CAKE
[1860]

Take five pounds of the finest flour dried and sifted, three pounds of fresh butter, five pounds of picked and washed currants dried before the fire,* two pounds of loaf-sugar, two nutmegs, quarter of an ounce of mace, half a quarter of an ounce of cloves, all finely beaten and sifted, sixteen eggs, whites and yolks kept separate, one pound of blanched almonds pounded with orange-flower water, one pound each of candied citron, orange and lemon-peel cut in neat slices. Mix these ingredients in the following manner: Begin working the butter with the hand till it becomes of a cream-like consistency, then beating in the sugar; for at least ten minutes whisk the whites of the eggs to a complete froth, and mix in with the butter and sugar; next, well beat up the yolks for full ten minutes, and adding them to the flour, nutmegs, mace, and cloves, continue beating the whole together for half an hour, or longer,† till wanted for the oven; then mix in lightly the currants, almonds, and candied peels, with the addition of a gill each of mountain wine and brandy; and, having lined a hoop‡ with paper, rub it well with butter, fill in the mixture, and bake it in a tolerably quick oven, taking care, however, not by any means to burn the cake, the top of which may be covered with paper. It is generally iced over on coming out of the oven, but without having any ornament on the top, so as to appear of a delicate plain, white.

* Plumped.
† This amount of beating ensured that the cake was "light." Yeast did not become available commercially until 1868; however, baking powder and baking soda were available by the date of this recipe, as was home-made yeast.
‡ Hoop = a type of round cake pan.

CHRISTMAS CAKE*
[1862 AND 1863]

To two pounds of flour well sifted unite
Of loaf-sugar ounces sixteen;
Two pounds of fresh butter, with eighteen fine eggs,
And four pounds of currants washed clean;

Eight ounces of almonds well blanched and cut small,
 The same-weight of citron sliced;
Of orange and lemon-peel candied one pound,
 And a gill of pale brandy uniced;
A large nutmeg grated: exact half an ounce
 Of allspice, but only a quarter
Of mace, coriander, and ginger well ground,
 Or pounded to dust in a mortar.
An important addition is cinnamon, which
 Is better increased than diminished;
The fourth of an ounce is sufficient. Now this
 May be baked four good hours till finished.

* I call this my Christmas currant cake and have been
baking it for more than ten years. Friends and rela-
tives look forward to their currant cake each
Christmas. Initially I had to estimate amounts to use.
I made several changes (e.g., powdered cloves for
coriander) and doubled the amount of liquor. The
whole recipe makes around 24 pounds—L.M.S.

CORNUCOPIAS
[1864]

I presume that most lady readers will have seen a pretty
dish for the sweet course composed of small cornu-
copias, filled with whipped cream; but as all may not
know how these are made, I hope the receipt for them
may not be unwelcome. Mix in a basin one-quarter of a
pound of fine white sifted sugar and two ounces of
flour, break two perfectly fresh eggs into this, and beat

it well. Rub a little white wax on your baking sheet, take about a dessert spoonful of the mixture and spread it in a round on your tin.* Bake these three minutes, take each off with a knife, and, as you do so, carefully roll each, at the oven's mouth, into a jelly bag of cornucopia shape. Dry them a little before the fire after they are rolled, fill them with pink or white whipped cream,† and send them to table on a nicely-folded napkin. They will keep for some time, if placed in a tin box in a dry place, without the cream, which must be put in fresh when they are to be served up.

> * That is, drop on greased tin by the tablespoonful.
> † Use creme chantilly or any desired cream filling.

FRUIT CAKE
[1864]

Two and a half cups dried apples stewed until soft; add one cup of sugar; stew a while longer, and chop the mixture, to which add one half cup of cold coffee, one of sugar, two eggs, a half cup of butter, one nutmeg, one teaspoonful of soda, and cinnamon and spices to taste.*

> * This recipe needs about 2 cups of flour
> to hold it together.

GERMAN CAKES
[1864]

Beat up four eggs, beat into them half a pound of butter, melted until it becomes liquid, a pint and a half of warm milk, and a teacupful of yeast.* Stir in as much flour as will make the mixture stiff; then tie it loosely in a cloth, put it into a pail of water, and leave it there until it rises to the top. Take the dough out of the cloth, mix with it three-quarters of a pound of sugar, the same of raisins (stoned), chopped lemon-peel, citron, and almonds, and divide it into cakes two inches across. Place these cakes on tins, and bake them.

* One package dry yeast.

HARRISON CAKE*
[1863]

Two cups of molasses, one cup of butter, one cup sugar, one cup sour cream, one teaspoonful cloves, one of saleratus, two teacups currants. Butter melted with molasses and poured into three or four cups of flour; then add sugar and half the cream; put in the rest of the cream when you have dissolved the saleratus in it. Then take enough more flour to make it about as thick as cup cakes; stir it ten or fifteen minutes, add the currants, and bake it in pans like cup cake.

*This cake may have been named for
President William Henry Harrison of
"Tippecanoe and Tyler too" (1841).
During his presidential campaign a large rally
in Ohio featured such foods as corn dodgers,
hard cider, and barbecued ham (Weaver, 1989).

INDIAN LOAF CAKE
[1860]

One pound of Indian meal, quarter of a pound of butter, two eggs, half a pound of sugar, quarter of a pound of raisins, and quarter of a pound of currants. Cut the butter into the Indian meal, and pour over it as much boiling milk as will make a thick batter; beat the eggs very light, and, when the batter is cool, stir them in; stone the raisins, wash, pick, and dry the currants; mix the raisins and currants together, and dredge as much wheat flour on them as will adhere to them, stir the fruit into the batter, and add the sugar. Bake it in a moderate oven two hours.

JEFFERSON CAKE
[1865]

Butter one pound, sugar one pound, flour two pounds, a little salt, soda quarter of an ounce, one grated nutmeg, a little cinnamon, and milk sufficient to form a dough. Cut into cakes, and bake.

LEMON CAKE
[1864]

[Sponge]

Beat six eggs, the yolks and whites separately, till in a solid froth; add to the yolks the grated rind of a fine lemon and six ounces of sugar dried and sifted; beat this a quarter of an hour; shake in with the left hand six ounces of dried flour; then add the whites of the eggs and the juice of the lemon; when these are well beaten in, put it immediately into tins, and bake it about an hour in a moderately hot oven.

LEMON GINGERBREAD
[1860]

Grate the rinds of two or three lemons, and add the juice to a glass of brandy; then mix the grated lemon in one pound of flour, make a hole in the flour, pour in half a pound of treacle, half a pound of butter melted, the lemon-juice, and brandy, and mix all up together with half an ounce of ground ginger and quarter of an ounce of Cayenne pepper.

LINCOLN CAKE
[1865]

Two eggs, two cups of sugar, a half cup of butter, one of sweet milk, three of flour, one teaspoonful of cream of tartar, half a teaspoonful of soda, and one of lemon essence.

OLD-FASHIONED CONNECTICUT WEDDING-CAKE
[1863]

Four pounds of sifted flour, two pounds of butter, two-and-three-quarters pounds of sugar, two cents' worth of yeast,* eight eggs, glass of white brandy, raisins, citron, mace, nutmeg, and any other spice to the taste.

Directions for Mixing.—Take all the flour, half the sugar, a little milk, and all the yeast, and mix like biscuit dough. When perfectly light, add the rest of the butter, and sugar, with eight eggs and set it to rise again. When light the second time, add the spice and brandy, and half a teaspoon of soda mixed well. Paper and butter the tins, and let it stand in them half an hour. Bake in a quick oven. This will make six loaves. It is much improved by frosting.

* Probably two cakes of compressed yeast or
two packages of active dry yeast.

OLD CONNECTICUT ELECTION CAKE*
[1863]

Eighteen pounds of flour, nine pounds good brown sugar (it makes this kind of cake more moist), nine pounds butter, ten eggs, three pints fresh yeast (distillery or homemade), nine pints new milk, two ounces nutmeg, two ounces mace, some cinnamon if liked (cinnamon is not in the original receipt—it can be added in any; I usually put it in), nine pounds of raisins. Currants and citron may be added, if one please; but usually currants are not used in this. Eight wineglasses each of sherry or Madeira wine and brandy. Currant wine will not do in cake. It makes it heavy.

These quantities will make eighteen or twenty loaves, and as it is too much for an ordinary family, I have reduced the quantity of Election Cake, which will make four large-sized loaves.

A Small Quantity of Election Cake.—Two and a quarter pounds flour, eighteen ounces butter, eighteen ounces sugar, a gill and a half of good fresh yeast, four and a half gills of new milk, two nutmegs, two eggs, half an ounce mace, two pounds raisins (stoned and chopped a little), one wineglass of sherry or Madeira wine, one ditto of brandy. In every kind of cake as much fruit can be used as one chooses.

Directions for Making These Cakes.—The night previous to baking, take all the flour, and all the yeast, and all the milk (if warmed from the cow it is sufficient, if not, must be warmed some), part of the sugar and part of the butter. Work it well together, and turn a pan over it and let it rise. In the morning it will be light. Then take the remainder of the sugar, butter, spices, liquor and eggs, and work well together, as for some other cake, then put it all into the cake; put togeth-er the night before, and beat it well 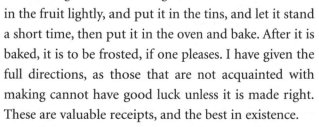 together for some time. Cover it, and let it rise again. After it is light, work in the fruit lightly, and put it in the tins, and let it stand a short time, then put it in the oven and bake. After it is baked, it is to be frosted, if one pleases. I have given the full directions, as those that are not acquainted with making cannot have good luck unless it is made right. These are valuable receipts, and the best in existence.

Judgment must be used in all cake making, and these cakes must not be kept too warm or too cold.

They are often kept too warm; that makes the butter oily, and scalds the whole and makes it sour, and the fault is in the receipt. There is no fault in these.

* According to one source (*Yankee*, March 1993), election cake is thought to have originated in Dorchester, Massachusetts, in 1820, when Otis Shepard and his sons served a version of this cake to every voter. The practice spread to other states and later the cake became known as Hartford Election Cake or, as here, Connecticut Election Cake. There is a recipe for "Election cake" in Amelia Simmons's *American Cookery,* which was published in 1796 (Fordyce, 1987).

MISSISSIPPI CAKE
[1860]

One pint of the best yellow cornmeal, a pint of buttermilk, two tablespoonfuls of melted butter, two eggs, a teaspoonful of salt, and a teaspoonful of saleratus.

QUEEN CAKE*
[1860 AND 1862]

Mix one pound of dried flour, the same of sifted sugar and of washed currants; wash one pound of butter in rose-water, beat it well, then mix with it eight eggs, yolks and whites beaten separately, and put in the dry ingredients by degrees; beat the whole an hour; butter little tins, teacups, or saucers, filling them only half full; sift a little fine sugar over just as you put them into the oven.

* An old traditional English cake, this is always a small currant cake and usually heart-shaped.

SNOW CAKE
[1865]

[A Genuine Scotch Receipt]

One pound of arrowroot, quarter pound of pounded white sugar, half pound of butter, and whites of six eggs; flavoring to taste, of essence of almonds, or vanilla, or lemon. Beat the butter into a cream; stir in the sugar and arrowroot gradually, at the same time beating the mixture. Whisk the whites of the eggs to a stiff froth, add them to the other ingredients, and beat well for twenty minutes. Put in whichever of the above flavoring may be preferred; pour the cake into a buttered mould or tin, and bake it in a moderate oven for one to one and a half hour.

VERMONT CURRANT CAKE
[1862]

One cup of butter, one of sweet milk, one of currants, three of sugar, four of flour, four eggs, one teaspoonful cream tartar, half teaspoonful soda, nutmeg, lemon, or vanilla. Made sometimes with less sugar.

WASHINGTON CAKE*
[1862 AND 1865]

Beat together one and a half pound of sugar, and three-quarters of a pound of butter; add four eggs well beaten, half a pint of sour milk, and one teaspoonful of saleratus, dissolved in a little hot water. Stir in gradually one and three-quarter pound of flour, one wineglassful of wine or brandy, and one nutmeg, grated. Beat all well together.

This will make two round cakes. It should be baked in a quick oven, and will take from fifteen to thirty minutes, according to the thickness of the cakes.

> * Often called Washington Pie, this is basically
> a cream pie like Boston Cream Pie, but the layers
> are usually separated with raspberry jam
> rather than custard.

I C I N G S

ALMOND ICING FOR A BRIDE CAKE
[1860]

Beat the whites of three eggs to a strong froth, beat a pound of almonds very fine with rose-water, mix them, with the eggs, lightly together; put in by degrees a pound of common loaf-sugar in powder. When the cake is baked enough, take it out, and lay on the icing, then put it in to brown.

ICING FOR RICH CAKES
[1864]

[An Ornamental Icing]

Put the whites of three or four eggs into a deep glazed pan, quite free from the least grease, and mix in gradually one pound of good loaf-sugar that has been powdered and sifted through a lawn sieve, till it is as thick as good rich cream; then beat it up with a wooden spoon until it becomes thick; add the juice of a lemon, strained and beat it again till it hangs to the spoon; then, with the spoon, drop some on the top of the cake, and with a clean knife smooth it well over the top and sides, about an eighth of an inch thick; then put it in a dry place, and it will be dry in a few hours. Ornament it while wet, if it is required to be ornamented, by sticking figures of sugar or plaster on it, or candied peel or angelica.

BISCUITS [COOKIES] AND CONFECTIONS

ALMOND CAKES [COOKIES]
[1864]

One pound of flour, half a pound of loaf-sugar, quarter of a pound of butter, two ounces of bitter almonds,* pounded in a small quantity of brandy, and two eggs. The cakes are not to be rolled, but made as rough as possible with a fork.

> * Bitter almonds contain the poison
> prussic acid and are not available here.
> Substitute sliced natural almonds.

ARROWROOT BISCUITS [COOKIES]
[1863 AND 1865]

Put together three-quarters of a pound of sugar, and the same weight of butter; beat three eggs well and mix with it, then stir in two cups of sifted arrowroot,* and two of flour; roll them thin, cut them with a biscuit-cutter; place them in buttered tins, and bake in a slow oven.

* This amount of arrowroot seems excessive and
would be much too expensive to use today,
but substituting flour or cornstarch would
alter the recipe too much.

CRACKNELS
[1861]

One pound of flour, half a pound of currants, half a pound of sugar, half a pound of butter, and a little cream; season with a little mace, and add as many eggs as will make the whole into a rather stiff paste. Make it up in round balls, or pull together with a fork, and dip them (before baking) in rough-pounded loaf-sugar.

FLORENTINES*
[1865]

[*Florentine Meringue*]

Roll puff paste to the thickness of the eighth of an inch, and lay it on a thin baking-tin. Spread over it a layer of greengage† or any other preserve or jam, and bake it in a moderate oven. Take it out, and when partially cool, having whipped some whites of eggs with sugar, put the whip over the preserve, and strew some minced almonds all over the surface, finishing with sifted sugar. Put it once more into the oven until the whip is quite stiff. The florentines should be of a pale color, and a few minutes after the paste is finally removed from the oven it should be cut into diamonds and served up.

* This is for Florentine *meringue* cookies or a "pastry dessert," but there is also another Florentine cookie recipe with many variations, especially one that is called "The Salzburg Florentine."
† A type of plum.

GINGERBREAD NUTS
[1860]

Two pounds of flour, one and a quarter pound of molasses, half a pound of sugar,* two ounces of ginger, ¾ lb. of butter (melted), and a small quantity of Cayenne pepper. The above to be mixed together and rolled out about the thickness of half an inch, or not quite so much, to be cut into cakes, and baked in a moderate oven.

* Brown sugar.

GERMAN FLOTTRENGEL
[1865]

Take one pound of dry flour, three-quarters of a pound of well-washed butter, ten tablespoonsful of cream. For the top of these cakes melted butter or egg, powdered sugar and cinnamon. Break the butter into small pieces, and mix with the flour, then adding the cream; mix quickly into a light paste. From this break pieces, and roll them out with the hand about a quarter of a yard long, and join the two ends in the middle, to give the form of a B. When all are done, grease them on top with egg or melted butter, strewing sugar and cinnamon over it. Those who like almonds will find them with the above very delicious. These cakes require to be baked quickly.

JUMBLES*
[1860 AND 1863]

Rasp on sugar, rinds of two lemons; dry, reduce to powder, and sift it with as much more as will make one pound. Mix it with one pound of flour, four well-beaten eggs, and six ounces warm butter. Drop the mixture on buttered tins, and bake in a very slow oven, for twenty or thirty minutes. Should look pale but be perfectly crisp.

* The dictionary says that a *jumble* is a small, thin, usually ring-shaped sugared cake, and the name is still used in some cookbooks (such as *Fannie Farmer*), but modern versions bear little resemblance to this recipe. A recipe for jumbles can be found in an English cookbook published in 1615.

ROUT DROPS*
[1862]

Mix two pounds of flour, one pound of butter, one pound of sugar, one pound of currants clean and dry;

then wet into a stiff paste, with two eggs, a large spoonful of orange-flower water, the same each of rose-water,
sweet wine, and brandy; drop on a tin plate floured. A
very short time bakes them.

> * A *rout* was a fashionable gathering or large evening
> party popular in the late eighteenth and early nine-
> teenth centuries. Rout Drops were probably made for
> very special social gatherings or receptions. The use
> of the very delicate flavorings of rosewater and
> orange-flower water suggests this possibility.

SEED CAKE*
[1860]

One cup of butter, two of white sugar, three eggs, half a
cup of seeds,† flour enough to make stiff; roll very thin
with sugar instead of flour. Bake quick. A very delicate
cake is made by substituting lemon for seeds.

> * The term *cake* was often used interchangeably for
> breads and cookies as well as cakes.
> †Use caraway seeds.

SHORT-BREAD
[1864]

For making good Scotch short-bread provide two
pounds of flour, one pound of butter, four eggs,* and
twelve ounces of loaf-sugar, powdered very finely. Rub
the butter and sugar into the flour with your hand, and,
by means of the eggs, convert it into a stiff paste. This

must be rolled out to quite half an inch in thickness and cut into square cakes, or round, if preferred. The Scotch ones are generally square, and six inches in size. The edges should be pinched up to the height of about an inch, and on the top of the cake should be laid some slices of candied peel and some large caraway comfits. These are slightly pressed down so as to imbed about half of each in the cake. They must be baked in a warm oven upon iron plates.

* Many old Scottish recipes do not contain eggs. Originally Scottish shortbread was probably a large round (not square) cake. Although previously always decorated, today it is usually decorated only for special occasions. Several different versions of shortbread recipes appeared in *Godey's*.

TEXAS CREAM CAKE [COOKIES]
[1860]

Rub together one quart of flour and two cups of sugar; add one tablespoonful of powdered orange-peel or a grated nutmeg; beat three eggs very light, and add them to half a pint of cream and half a glass of milk; add these ingredients to the flour and sugar, and beat them all well together; add another quart of flour, and make it into a stiff dough; knead, but do not roll it, and make it into little biscuits with your hands. They are light and nice; try them.

SOFT COOKIES*
[1864]

Take one coffee-cup of butter, three of sugar, one of thick cream, and four eggs; mix the butter and sugar, then add the eggs and the cream. Take a pint of sifted flour and a teaspoonful of soda; mix well and stir into the other ingredients sufficient of it to make the paste or dough stiff enough to roll out; cut it in squares, impress with a fancy mould, and bake in a slow oven. Caraway seed and ground coriander seed are often used to flavor these biscuits called "cookies."

* In the United States the word *cookie* apparently came from the Dutch word for cake (koek). This seems to be a version of a cookie recipe found in a 1796 American cookbook.

CANDIED ORANGE OR LEMON-PEEL
[1862]

Take the fruit, cut it lengthwise, remove all the pulp and interior skin, then put the peel into strong salt and water for six days; then boil them in spring water until they are soft, and place them in a sieve to drain; make a thin syrup with a pound of sugar candy to a quart of water; boil them in it for half an hour, or till they look clear; make a thick syrup with sugar and as much water as will melt it; put in the peel, and boil them over a slow fire until the syrup candies in the pan; then take them out, powder pounded sugar over them, and dry them before the fire in a cool oven.

DESSERTS

AN APPLE ISLAND
[1865]

Make some good apple-sauce, which has been flavored
with lemon and clove; beat it up very fine with loaf-sugar
enough to taste sweet; add two glasses of sherry; then
beat the whites of four eggs separately till they are of a
light froth;* strain them into a large basin; beat them up
again; now add two tablespoonfuls of cream or a little
milk, and a quarter of an ounce of isinglass† dissolved in
a little water, and add to the milk and egg froth; beat it
well up; take off the froth with a spoon, and lay it on an
inverted sieve over a dish; when sufficient froth is made,
beat the remainder up with the apples till the whole is
very light and frothy; place the apples piled high in a glass
dish; pour some cold custard round out on it; then take
off the froth, and put on top of the apples.

* Like a meringue.
† Substitute plain gelatin.

APPLE SNOW-BALLS
[1863]

Take a half a dozen fresh apples, cut them into quarters and carefully remove the cores from them; then put them together, having introduced into the cavity caused by the removal of the cores, two cloves and a thin slice of lemon-rind into each apple. Have at hand half a dozen damp cloths, upon each dispose of a liberal layer of clean, picked rice; place each apple in an upright position in the middle of the grain, and draw the sides of the cloths containing the rice over the same, tying them at the top only sufficiently tight to admit of its swelling whilst under the operation of boiling—three quarters of an hour will suffice. When released from the cloths they will resemble snow-ball. Open, add sugar, butter, and nutmeg to the fruit, and serve them up to table. The above will be found very wholesome and satisfactory food for children.

BROWN CHARLOTTE PUDDING*
[1863]

Butter a pudding mould well, and line it with thin slices of bread and butter. These slices must be cut neatly, and the crust at the edges removed. Take some good baking apples, and cut them as for dumplings, fill the mould with them, putting in between the quarters some slices of candied lemon-peel, a little grated nutmeg, and some sugar. Cover it with bread on which there is plenty of butter, put a small plate on top of the mould, and bake it for three hours.

* Today charlotte molds are lined with lady fingers, sponge cake, or Génoise, but in the nineteenth century buttered plain bread was used.

SALADE D'ORANGES
[1862]

Delicious for dessert. Peel and slice six large oranges, and arrange them in a dessert centre dish, with powdered loaf-sugar sprinkled over every layer. Add some Madeira wine, and sprinkle white sugar over all the moment before it is served.

ORANGE PUDDING
[1860 AND 1865]

Take four fine oranges,* which soak in boiling water ten minutes, grate off the outside rind, which divide into two portions. Mix one portion with two tablespoonfuls of flour and half an ounce of pounded loaf-sugar, rub in two ounces of dripping or butter. Make a thin batter with two tablespoonfuls of milk, the yolks of two eggs, and white of one. Cut your fruit in slices, having first freed it from the inner white peel, strew with the remaining portion of grated peel and white powdered sugar, alternately a layer of each. Two ounces of sugar are generally sufficient. Pour the batter over, and bake in a moderate oven from twenty minutes to half an hour.

* Oranges were not easily accessible until the
late 1800s when they began to be shipped from
California and Florida, and special serving
dishes were invented for them.

TO PRESERVE PIPPINS IN SLICES
[1862]

Take the fairest pippins, pare them, and cut them in slices a quarter of an inch thick, without taking out the cores; boil two or three lemons, and slice them with the apples; take the same weight of white sugar (or clarified brown sugar), put half a gill of water for each pound of sugar, dissolve it, and set it over the fire; when it is boiling hot, put in the slices, let them boil very gently until they are clear, then take them with a skimmer, and spread them out on flat dishes to cool; boil the syrup until it is quite thick, and pour it over them. These may be done a day before they are wanted; two hours will be sufficient to make a fine dish for dessert or supper.

RHUBARB FOOL*
[1863]

Boil a quart or more of rhubarb, nicely peeled, and cut into pieces an inch long. Pulp through a sieve, sweeten, and let it stand to cool. Put a pint of cream, or new milk, into a stew-pan with a stick of cinnamon, a small piece of lemon-peel, a few cloves, corriander-seeds, and sugar to taste; boil ten minutes. Beat up the yolks of four eggs, and a little flour; stir into the cream, set it over the fire till it boils, stirring all the time; remove, and let it stand till cold. Mix the fruit and cream together, and add a little grated nutmeg.

* "Fool" is a dish of crushed fruit with whipped cream and sugar. The name comes from the French word "fouler," which means "to crush".

ALMOND PUDDING
[1863]

Beat in a mortar half a pound of sweet, and a very few bitter almonds* with a spoonful of water; then mix four ounces of butter, four eggs (which should be well beaten), two spoonfuls of cream, and one of brandy; nutmeg and sugar to taste. (The brandy should be warmed with the butter.) Butter some cups well, and fill them half-full with the above mixture. Bake them thoroughly, and serve with butter, wine and sugar.

* Bitter almonds are not available in this country; substitute 1 teaspoon almond extract.

COFFEE CREAM
[1864]

This is a delicate and agreeable dish for an evening entertainment. Dissolve one ounce and a quarter of isinglass* in half a pint of water. Boil for two hours a teacupful of *whole* coffee [beans] in about half a pint of water (ground coffee is not so good for the purpose); add a teacupful to the melted isinglass. Put them into a saucepan with half a pint of milk, and let the whole boil up; sweeten with loaf-sugar, and let it stand ten minutes  to cool, then add a pint of good cream; stir it well up, and pour it into a mould, and put it into a cool place to fix;† turn out on a glass dish before serving up.

* Substitute plain gelatin.
†To set and chill.

COTTAGE PUDDING*
[1863 AND 1864]

Three cups flour, one cup sugar, one cup milk, two table-spoonfuls butter, two teaspoonfuls cream tartar, one egg; beat all together, then add one teaspoonful soda; flavor with lemon. Bake one-half hour; serve with sauce.
Sauce:—One cup butter, two cups powdered sugar beaten to a cream, two tablespoons wine, half spoonful vanilla beaten with it, half pint boiling water.

* Although this was one of its first appearances in print, this recipe (almost exactly) can be found in some cookbooks today. *Fannie Farmer's* suggests serving it with either vanilla or hard sauce.

A DELICATE PUDDING
[1861]

[Baked Custard]

The yelks of five eggs beat very well, half a pound of pounded sugar, half a pint of milk, a slice of butter warmed in the milk, and a tablespoonful of flour. The sauce should be made of one glass of sherry, a little loaf sugar, and melted butter. Bake the puddings in large teacups, turn them out, and pour the sauce over them.

THE HELENA PUDDING
[1862]

[Baked Custard]

Pour one pint of boiling milk upon three ounces of grated bread, one quarter of butter,* four eggs, leaving out two of the whites, the rind of a large lemon, sugar to your taste. Place any sort of preserve at the bottom of a tart-dish; pour the above over and bake it.

* Quarter of a pound.

HERODOTUS PUDDING*
[1861]

Half a pound of bread crumbs, half a pound of best figs, six ounces of suet, six ounces of brown sugar; mince the figs and suet very nicely; a little salt, two eggs well beaten, nutmeg to your taste; boil in a mould four hours. Serve with a wine sauce.

* This pudding presumably was named for
Herodotus because it is made with figs and
served with wine sauce.

INDIAN PUDDING*
[1863]

Two quarts of boiling milk, with Indian meal enough to make a thin batter: stir in while boiling hot. Add sugar, allspice, to your taste; also a teacup of cold milk. Bake five hours in a moderate oven.

* This very traditional and popular dessert in
nineteenth-century New England is still enjoyed
today. Indian Pudding was one of the foods
that received favorable comments from Union soldier
correspondents and diarists (Wiley, 1952).

JENNY LIND'S PUDDING*
[1862]

Grate the crums of half a loaf, butter and dish well, and lay in a thick layer of the crums; pare ten or twelve apples, cut them down, and put a layer of them and sugar; then crums alternately, until the dish is full; put a bit of butter on the top, and bake it in an oven or American reflector. An excellent and economical pudding.

* The Swedish Nightingale had toured the United
States in 1850. Other dishes were also named for her,
in particular a French consommé.

UNION PUDDING*
[1865]

Take one cup of white sugar, three tablespoonfuls of flour, two eggs, one grated nutmeg, and one good-sized cocoanut grated fine, two teacupfuls of new milk and a tablespoonful of good fresh butter. Bake like tarts without an upper crust.

* Recipes were often given political names, and this is probably an example.

MADEIRA CREAM
[1863 AND 1865]

Take seven or more sponge-cakes, split them in halves, line a glass dish with the pieces; mix together two wineglassfuls of Madeira wine or Sherry, and one wineglassful of brandy; with a teaspoon pour a little of this mixture over the layer of pieces; on this again put a layer of raspberry jelly, which can readily be made by putting a pot of raspberry jam in the oven; in a few minutes it will be warm, when the liquid, which is the jelly, can be strained from it, and poured over the pieces. Now put the other layer of pieces, soak this with wine as before, but omit the raspberry. Make a custard as directed for boiled custard;* when cold, and just as the dish is going to table, pour the cold custard over, and sprinkle some ratafias on top.

* Use Thun Pudding sauce on page 230.

PLUM PUDDINGS*
[1862]

In the making of plum puddings, the following results of the examination and comparison of eighteen receipts may be usefully studied and applied:—

Average of Eighteen Receipts for Plum Pudding.

Fine flour, half a pound; bread-crumbs, quarter of a pound; suet, three quarters of a pound; eggs (yolk and white), four; mixed dried fruit, one pound and a half; mixed liquid, a third of a pint. . . .

The average time for ingredients weighing four pounds is about four hours.

* *Godey's* published numerous recipes for plum puddings, usually in December issues. This was an attempt to arrive at an average recipe.

RICH PLUM PUDDING*
[1863 AND 1864]

Stone carefully one pound of the best raisins, wash and pick one pound of currants, chop very small one pound of fresh beef suet, blanch and chop small or pound two ounces of sweet almonds and once ounce of bitter ones,† mix the whole well together, with one pound of sifted flour, and the same weight of crumb of bread soaked in milk, then squeezed dry and stirred with a spoon until reduced to a mash, before it is mixed with the flour. Cut in small pieces two ounces each of preserved citron, orange, and lemon-peel, and add a quarter of an ounce of mixed spice; quarter of a pound of moist sugar should be put into a basin, with eight eggs, and well beaten together with a three-pronged fork; stir this with the pudding, and make it of the proper consistence with milk. Remember that it must not be made too thin, or the fruit will sink to the bottom, but be made to the consistence of good thick batter. Two wineglassfuls of brandy should be poured over the fruit and space, mixed together in a basin, and allowed to stand three or four hours before the pudding is made, stirring them occasionally. It must be tied in a cloth, and will take five hours of constant boiling. When done, turn it out on a dish, sift loaf-sugar over the top, and serve it with wine-sauce‡ in a boat, and some poured round the pudding.

The pudding will be of considerable size, but half the quantity of materials, used in the same proportion, will be equally good.

* Plum pudding can be traced to the time of William the Conqueror, who reportedly rewarded the cook who invented it with a manor in Surrey.
† Use one teaspoon almond extract.
‡ See page 231.

SOUFFLÉE PUDDING*
[1863]

Take two ounces of sugar, four ounces of flour, two ounces of fresh butter, the yelks of three eggs well beaten, the whites also, but beaten separately, a tablespoonful of orange juice. Beat the whole together, strain it into a pie-dish, which must be filled only half full, and bake for half an hour in a very quick, sharp oven.

* This recipe is unusual for its use of orange juice.

THUN* PUDDING
[1865]

Chop very small two ounces almonds, and some lemon-peel; put them in a saucepan with a pint of milk, and sugar to taste; when this begins to boil, stir in slowly a large cupful of ground rice, and let it boil ten minutes, stirring the whole time. Pour in a mould, and when cold turn out. (Sauce): Put two ounces white sugar in a pan, with a little water, stir until melted and become a light golden brown; add a pint of milk, bring this to a boil, then strain it, and add the yelks of four eggs; put the strained milk and eggs on the fire and stir until it thickens; when this is cold, pour it round the pudding.

* Thun is a town in central Switzerland
on the Aar River.

PUDDING SAUCES
[1862]

Common Wine Sauce.—Make thin a few ounces of melted butter, then add from a tablespoon to two of coarsely pounded lump sugar, and a glass of sherry with half a glass of brandy; a little grated lemon-peel or nutmeg, or both together, are improvements.

Burnt Cream Sauce.—Put two ounces of sifted sugar on the fire in a small saucepan, stir it, and when quite brown pour slowly in a gill of thin cream, stirring it all the time. To be used as a sauce to custard or batter pudding.

Sweet Pudding Sauce Without Wine is made with melted butter, a little cream added, sweetened to the palate, and flavored with nutmeg, cinnamon, or mace.

Plum Pudding Sauce.—Add to four ounces of melted butter, or thick arrowroot, an ounce and a half each of the following—viz.: sherry, French brandy, and curacao; sweeten to the taste, and add also a little nutmeg and lemon-peel grated.

Fruit Sauces are easily made for any plain puddings by stewing the fresh fruit with rather less sugar than for preserving, and adding water till they are of a proper consistency for a sauce. Some cooks mix a little arrowroot with the water, and then strain before serving.

Receipt for Ice Cream*
[1862]

There is nothing equal to pure cream, for the making of a superior article of ice cream, although a very good article is made from milk, by adding other ingredients to enrich it and give it the proper consistency. For this purpose eggs are frequently used, and sometimes good Bermuda arrowroot or similar substances. Thin cream or milk should have more sugar. As a general rule, six ounces of sugar to one quart of cream. The following receipt is recommended as a substitute for pure cream:

One quart of rich milk, two fresh eggs, six ounces of white sugar, and three teaspoonfuls of Bermuda arrowroot; the arrowroot, if used, should be rubbed smooth in a little cold milk. Beat the eggs and sugar together, bring the milk to the boiling point, but do not let it boil, then stir in the arrowroot, and remove it from the fire, adding immediately the eggs and sugar, at the same time keep stirring briskly to prevent the eggs from cooking; then set aside to cool. If flavored with extracts, it should be done just before it is put in the freezer.

Vanilla should be boiled in a little water; but a better method is to boil the bean, or keep it steeped in water in a bottle well corked, or other closed vessel, immersed a day or longer in hot water. Then add white sugar to form a thick syrup which can be used at pleasure.

> * Commercial ice cream had been available in United States since around 1780, but the ice cream freezer was not invented until 1846. Its small size made it very popular for home use. *Godey's* maintained that ice cream was practically a necessity of life.

CURRANT ICE CREAM
[1862]

Put one large spoonful and a half of currant jelly into a basin with half a gill of syrup, squeeze in one lemon and a half, add a pint of cream and a little cochineal,* then pass it through a sieve and finish in a general way.

> * Substitute red food coloring.

FROZEN CUSTARD
[1860]

Take one quart of milk, five eggs, and a half pound of sugar; beat the eggs and sugar together; boil* the milk and pour it on to the eggs and sugar, beating it at the same time; put it on the fire again, and keep stirring to prevent its burning; soon as it thickens, take it off and strain it through a half sieve, when cool, add the flavor, and it is ready for freezing.

> * It is not necessary to boil milk today.

ORANGE OR PINEAPPLE ICE CREAM
[1860]

Cut the fruit into thin slices, covering the same with plenty of fine or pulverized white sugar. After standing several hours, the syrup may be drawn off and used for flavoring as described in the method of preparing vanilla for flavoring. [As instructed under recipe for ice cream.] The flavor of other fruits may be obtained in the same way.

PINE APPLE ICE CREAM
[1862]

Pare a ripe, juicy pine apple, chop it up fine, and pound it to extract the juice. Cover it with sugar and let it lie a while in a china bowl. When the sugar has entirely melted, strain the juice into a quart of good cream, and add a little less than a pound of loaf sugar. Beat up the cream and freeze it in the same manner as common ice cream.

EXCELLENT STRAWBERRY ICE CREAM
[1862]

Pass a pint of picked strawberries through a sieve with wooden spoon, add four ounces of powdered sugar, and a pint of cream, and freeze.

GLOSSARY

American reflector: A spitted oven rack on which meat, fowl, fish, or fruit could be roasted before the fire.

apron: A thick fold of skin.

arrowroot: A light starch used in puddings, pie fillings, and dessert mixtures. It is made from the rootstock of a tropical plant that was first grown in the West Indies and is now cultivated in nearly all tropical countries.

ash-pone: A coarse corn bread baked in ashes, made chiefly in the South.

baking powder: Introduced in 1856, it combined saleratus (baking soda) and cream of tartar and was a great convenience to housewives.

balm: Any of the various aromatic plants of the genus *Melissa.*

bannock: A cake of Indian meal fried in lard (from the Scottish bread baked in flat loaves).

barding: Covering very lean birds with a layer of fat.

barm: The froth or foam rising on fermented malt liquors.

beards: The gills of certain bivalve mollusks.

beef dodger: A cornmeal cake filled with minced beef, popular in the South.

berries: The eggs of a crustacean.

bitter almond: A variety of the common almond having bitter kernels that yield a very poisonous oil (prussic acid). It is used as a flavoring in European countries but is not available in this country.

bouilli (French): Boiled.

brace: A pair of like things; for example, a brace of partridges.

bruise: To pound into fragments; crush.

capsicum: An herb or shrub of the nightshade family, including the common red pepper, that produces pods which are prepared as condiments or gastric stimulants; also called bird pepper.

carmine: A crimson pigment derived from cochineal.

carrageen: A dark purple cartilaginous seaweed that, when dried and bleached, is known as "Irish Moss" and is used in making blanc mange.

caudle: A warm drink of gruel with wine, eggs, sugar, and spices, for invalids.

caul: A membrane covering certain organs. It is being used more and more now for pâtés.

chalybeate: Impregnated with compounds of iron.

citron-melon: A large lemonlike fruit with a thick, firm peel or rind. The rind is preserved and candied for use in cakes and puddings. Fragrant oils are also taken from the rind.

clary flowers: The flowers of a species of sage.

cochineal: A brilliant scarlet dye prepared from the dried bodies of a female insect of tropical America and Java; used as a food coloring.

collar: To roll up and tie and cook with herbs and spices; to corn.

collop: A small portion or slice, especially of meat.

comfits and confitures: A sweetmeat or confection.

corn dodger: A cake of corn bread, shaped by hand and fried, baked, or boiled; popular in the South, where it was eaten with ham or greens.

corn pone: A southern corn bread often made without milk or eggs and shaped in an oval.

cracknel: A hard, brittle biscuit.

crude tartar: An acid substance deposited in grape juice during fermentation as a pinkish sediment: crude bitartrate of potassium.

Curacao: A liqueur flavored with the peel of the sour orange (after Curaçao, an island in the Caribbean).

dodger: *See* beef dodger; corn dodger.

empyreumatic: Fiery.

entremet: A side dish served in addition to the principal course.

esculent: Eatable or edible.

farinaceous: Made from, rich in, or consisting of starch.

fillip: To enhance, as, for example, with a sharp sauce for broiled meats.

fine: To clarify or clear.

fish slice: A knife with a broad or wedge-shaped blade used especially for serving food.

flip: A drink of beer, rum, and sugar.

frit (French, *fritte*): To fry.

gauffres: Waffles; honeycomb or wafflelike.

ghee: A butterlike substance made by melting, boiling, straining, and cooling the butterfat or buffalo milk in India, or a clarified butter.

gill: Liquid measure equal to ¼ pint or 0.118 liters.

gravy: Broth or stock.

green goose: A goose under four months of age.

griskin: The lean part of a loin of pork.

gum arabic: A gum from various species of acacia, used in medicine, candy, and ink.

hob: A projection at the backside of the interior of a fireplace that served as a shelf to keep things warm.

hog and hominy: A southern dish of pork and boiled corn, often a staple of the poor.

hogshead: In liquid measures, especially of wine, a large cask, especially one with a capacity of 63 to 140 gallons.

Indian meal: An older name for corn meal.

Indian pudding: A popular New England dessert made from cornmeal, milk, sugar, molasses, and spices.

isinglass: A preparation of nearly pure gelatin made from the swim bladders of certain fish.

lights: The lungs of animals, so called for their lightness in weight.

Lisbon sugar: A kind of soft sugar.

loaf sugar: A conical mass of concentrated sugar.

maigre: Scrawny, scanty, lean meat.

marbree (French, *marbre*): Marble.

milk-warm: Luke warm.

morellas: A cultivated cherry with dark, red skin, juice, and flesh.

nibs: Pointed parts or tips.

non pareil: A small flat chocolate disk covered with sugar pellets; also the sugar pellets themselves.

Noyeau: A liqueur with a brandy base flavored primarily with essential oils derived from kernels of peaches, plums, and cherries or from almonds, the predominant flavor being that of bitter almonds (from French, *noyau,* kernel or pit). All of these pits contain prussic acid.

orgeat: A flavoring syrup prepared with an emulsion of almonds, or formerly with a decoction of barley.

ottar (*also* attar): The fragrant essential oil extracted from the petals of flowers, especially roses.

pack thread: Strong thread or twine.

panada: A prepared dish containing soaked bread crumbs.

patna: A rice which originated in the Ganges area and is particularly noted for its elongated, firm grain.

pearlash: Commercial potassium carbonate (purified potash). It was discovered in the 1790s and used before the introduction of baking soda to make dough rise.

pinions: Wings.

pipkin: A small earthenware jar.

pottle: An old measure equal to a half gallon.

quartern (chiefly British): A fourth part of certain measures or weights; as a peck or pound; also, a four-pound loaf of bread.

race: Ginger root.

rape: Refuse stalks and skins of grapes in winemaking.

rasher: A strip of bacon; a slice or portion.

rasp: To grate or scrape.

ratafias: Any liqueur flavored with fruit kernels, especially of bitter almonds; also, a sweet, almond-flavored biscuit.

réchauffé (French): Food that has been reheated.

recherché (French): Refined, sought after, exotic, or rare.

remove (British): A dish or course at dinner removed to give place to another.

rissole: An entrée made of meat or fish chopped up and mixed with bread crumbs and egg, rolled up in cakes, and fried.

sago: The dried powder of East Indian palm used as a thickening agent in puddings.

salamander: A large poker or other implement used around or in fire or when red-hot.

saleratus: Soda bicarbonate (baking soda), introduced about 1840. It required the addition of cream of tartar to work.

salsify: A plant native to Europe having grasslike leaves, purple flowers, and an edible taproot that is eaten as a vegetable.

savoy: A large sponge cake often baked or cut in fancy shapes; also, a lady finger (from the Savoy region in France).

scrag-end: A lean or bony piece of meat.

sheep's trotters: The animal's feet.

sherbet: A refreshing drink made of diluted fruit juice.

shives: Slices cut off, as of bread.

sippets: A piece of toast or bread used to sop up gravy or sauce.

slice: Slotted spoon or spatula.

Smyrnas: Red Smyrnas were a type of raisin that made a rich, full-bodied wine. Black Smyrnas made a very strong-bodied wine. They were so called probably because of the geographical location, which in the mid-nineteenth century belonged to Greece.

sorrel: Any of several plants of the genus *Rumex* having acid-flavored leaves sometimes used as salad greens.

souse: To steep in a mixture, as in pickling.

spaddle: A small spade or other utensil, probably wooden.

sponge: A raised dough.

stir-about: A porridge made of oatmeal or cornmeal stirred in boiling water or milk.

tamarind: A tropical tree of the senna family. The fruit or pod has an acid pulp and is used for preserves and made into a cooling laxative drink.

treacle: Molasses.

trundle: A roll.

❧ REFERENCES ❧

Andrews, Eliza. "The Last March Home." In Walter Sullivan, ed., *The War the Women Lived: Female Voices from the Confederate South.* Nashville: J.S. Sanders, 1995.

Beeton, Mrs. Isabella. *Mrs. Beeton's Book of Household Management.* London: S.O. Beeton, 1859-61.

Billings, John D. *Hardtack and Coffee.* Boston: George M. Smith, 1887.

Burr, Virginia Ingraham. *The Secret Eye: The Journal of Ella Gertrude Clanton Thomas, 1848-1889.* Chapel Hill: Univ. of North Carolina Press, 1990.

Burroughs, Frances M. "The Confederate Receipt Book: A Study in Food Substitution in the American Civil War." *South Carolina Historical and Genealogical Magazine* 93 (Jan. 1992): 31-50.

Clark, Clifford E., Jr. "The Vision of the Dining Room." In *Dining in America, 1850-1900,* ed. Kathryn Grover. Amherst: Univ. of Massachusetts Press, 1987.

Clay-Clopton, Mrs. *A Belle of the Fifties, Memoirs of Mrs. Clay of Alabama, Covering Social and Political Life in Washington and the South, 1853-66.* New York: Doubleday, Page, 1905.

Confederate Receipt Book, The. Athens: Univ. of Georgia Press, 1960.

Fannie Farmer Cookbook, The. 11th ed. Rev. by Wilma Lord Perkins. Boston: Little, Brown, 1965.

FitzGibbon, Theodora. *The Food of the Western World.* New York: Quandrangle/New York Times, 1976.

Fordyce, Eleanor T. "Cookbooks of the 1800s." In *Dining in America, 1850-1900,* ed. Kathryn Grover. Amherst: Univ. of Massachusetts Press, 1987.

Godey's Lady's Book. Philadelphia, 1830-1898.

Grover, Kathryn, ed. *Dining in America, 1850-1900.* Amherst: Univ. of Massachusetts Press, 1987.

Hinman, William, comp. *Camp and Field.* Cleveland: Hamilton, 1892.

Hooker, Richard J. *Food and Drink in America: A History.* Indianapolis: Bobbs-Merrill, 1981.

Johnson, Sharon Peregrine, and Byron A. Johnson. *The Authentic Guide to Drinks of the Civil War Era, 1853-1873.* Gettysburg, Pa.: Thomas Publications, 1992.

McCarthy, Carlton. *Detailed Minutiae of Soldier Life in the Army of Northern Virginia, 1861-1865.* Richmond, Va.: 1882.

McCutcheon, Marc. *The Writer's Guide to Everyday Life in the 1800s.* Cincinnati: Writer's Digest Books, 1993.

McIntosh, Elaine N. *American Food Habits in Historical Perspective.* Westport, Conn.: Praeger, 1995.

McWhiney, Grady. *Cracker Culture.* Tuscaloosa: Univ. of Alabama Press, 1988.

Miller, David W. "Technology and the Ideal: Production Quality and Kitchen Reform in Nineteenth-Century America." In *Dining in America, 1850-1900,* ed. Kathryn Grover. Amherst: Univ. of Massachusetts Press, 1987.

Moore, J.N. *Confederate Commissary General.* Shippensburg, Pa.: White Mane, 1996.

Mussey, Barrows. *A Book of Country Things. Told by Walter Needham.* Brattleboro, Vt.: Stephen Greene Press, 1965.

Nofi, Alfred A. *A Civil War Treasury.* New York: Da Capo Press, 1995.

Oxford English Dictionary, 2nd ed. Oxford: Clarendon Pess, 1989.

Phillips, Ulrich Bonnell. *Life and Labor in the Old South.* Boston: Little, Brown, 1929.

Plante, Ellen M. *The American Kitchen, 1700 to the Present.* New York: Facts on File, 1995.

Porcher, Frances P. *Resources of the Southern Fields and Forests.* Charleston, S.C.: Evans & Cogswell, 1863.

Randolph, Mary. *The Virginia House-Wife.* 1824; rpt. in 1984 with Historical Notes and Commentaries by Karen Hess. Columbia, S.C.: Univ. of South Carolina Press, 1984.

Robertson, James I., Jr. *Soldiers Blue and Gray.* Columbia, S.C.: Univ. of South Carolina Press, 1988.

Roland, Charles P. *Louisiana Sugar Plantations during the American Civil War.* Leiden, Netherlands: E.J. Brill, 1957.

Rombauer, Irma, and Marion Rombauer Becker. *Joy of Cooking.* Indianapolis: Bobbs-Merrill, 1975.

Root, Waverly, and Richard de Rochemont. *Eating in America.* New York: William Morrow, 1976.

Rorabaugh, William J. "Beer, Lemonade, and Propriety in the Gilded Age." In *Dining in America, 1850-1900,* ed. Kathryn Grover. Amherst: Univ. of Massachusetts Press, 1987.

Smallzried, Kathleen Ann. *The Everlasting Pleasure.* New York: Appleton-Century-Crofts, 1956.

Wason, Betty. *Cooks, Gluttons and Gourmets*. Garden City, N.Y.: Doubleday, 1962.

Weaver, William W. *America Eats: Forms of Edible Folk Art*. New York: Museum of American Folk Art, 1989.

Wiley, Bell Irvin. *The Life of Billy Yank*. Indianapolis: Bobbs-Merrill, 1952.

————. *The Life of Johnny Reb*. Indianapolis: Bobbs-Merrill, 1943.

Williams, Susan. *Savory Suppers and Fashionable Feasts: Dining in Victorian America*. New York: Pantheon Books, 1985.

Wolcott, Imogene. *The Yankee Cookbook*. New York: Van Rees Press, 1939.

Yankee 57 (March 1993).